# ALLUSIONS TO SCRIPTURE IN THE PSALMS OF SOLOMON

## *Textual Tradition, Interpretation, and Historical Implications*

**Cahiers de Biblia Patristica**

Collection fondée par Pierre Maraval,
dirigée par Rémi Gounelle



1. *Lectures anciennes de la Bible*, 1987
2. *Figures de l'Ancien Testament chez les Pères*, 1989
3. *Figures du Nouveau Testament chez les Pères*, 1991
4. *Le Psautier chez les Pères*, 1994
5. *Le livre de Job chez les Pères*, 1996
6. *Rois et reines de la Bible au miroir des Pères*, 1999
7. *La résurrection chez les Pères*, 2003
8. J.-M. Prieur, *La croix chez les Pères*, 2006
9. *Le décalogue au miroir des Pères*, 2008
10. M. Cambe, *Avenir solaire et angélique des justes*, 2009
11. H. Agbenuti, *Didyme d'Alexandrie. Sens profond des Écritures et pneumatologie*, 2011
12. G. Aragione & R. Gounelle (éd.), *Soyez des changeurs avisés*, 2012
13. M. G. Bilby, *As the bandit will I confess you*, 2013
14. F. Vinel, *Les visions de l'Apocalypse*, 2014
15. S. M. Badilita & L. Mellerin (éd.), *Le miel des Écritures*, 2015
16. C. Mulard, *La pensée symbolique de Romanos le Mélode*, 2016
17. M. Stavrou & J. Van Rossum (éd.), *Écriture et tradition chez les Pères de l'Église*, 2017
18. L. Mellerin (éd.), *Le livre scellé*, 2017
19. R. Gounelle & J.-M. Vercruysse (éd.), *La destruction de Sodome et de Gomorrhe* (Gn 18-19) *dans la littérature chrétienne des premiers siècles*, 2018
20. G. Aragione (éd.), *Femmes de savoir et savoirs des femmes. Littérature et musique religieuses entre l'Antiquité tardive et le Moyen Âge*, 2019
21. R. Gounelle (éd.), *La Bible dans les catéchèses des* IV^e^-V^e^ *siècles*, 2020
22. L. Mellerin (éd.), *Le puits des eaux vives*, 2021
23. G. Bady (éd.), *La source sans fin, La Bible chez Jean Chrysostome*, 2021
24. R. Burnet *et al.* (éd.), *Du Jésus des Écritures au Christ des théologiens*, 2022

Publiés par le Centre d'Analyse et de Documentation Patristiques (rattaché à l'Unité de recherche 4378 « Théologie protestante »), les **Cahiers de Biblia Patristica** proposent des études sur l'utilisation des textes bibliques dans la littérature chrétienne des premiers siècles. Ils accueillent des monographies ou des ensembles d'articles sur un même texte ou thème biblique.

Cahiers de Biblia Patristica

25

Jan Joosten

# ALLUSIONS TO SCRIPTURE IN THE PSALMS OF SOLOMON

## *Textual Tradition, Interpretation, and Historical Implications*

BREPOLS

2024

Tous les volumes de cette collection sont évalués sur la base de critères académiques par le Comité de Rédaction, qui fonde son opinion sur des rapports rédigés par des critiques spécialistes dans le domaine. Le comité de rédaction garantit que l'appréciation est faite d'une manière indépendante et de façon à éviter les conflits d'intérêts.

La mise en pages de ce volume a été effectuée par Ersie Leria (Université de Strasbourg), à laquelle vont tous nos remerciements

Couverture et p. 5 : Portrait des Rois David et Salomon, in *The holy court*, five tomes, written in French by Nicholas Caussin…; translated into English by Sr. T. H. (Thomas Hawkins) and others, Londres, 1650; photography: Pitts Theological Library [https://dia.pitts.emory.edu/dia/book_details.cfm?ID=7386].



D/2024/0095/150
ISBN 978-2-503-61114-3
eISBN 978-2-503-61115-0
DOI 10.1484/M.CBP-EB.5.137051
ISSN 0982-3468
eISSN 2983-9351
Printed in the E.U. on acid-free paper.

DAVID. SOLOMON.

# Introduction

The Psalms of Solomon, a collection of 18 songs preserved in a small number of Greek manuscripts and attested also in a Syriac translation, do not seem to have been particularly popular ever. Although they are mentioned in the table of contents of the codex Alexandrinus of the fifth century, they are not really part of the Septuagint canon.[1] The earliest attested manuscripts are from the tenth century, most of them containing a collection of wisdom books: Proverbs, Ecclesiastes, Canticles, Wisdom, Job, Ben Sira—and Psalms of Solomon.[2] The songs are never quoted nor alluded to in any ancient ecclesiastic writer.[3]

---

1 See Henry B. Swete, *An Introduction to the Old Testament in Greek*, revised by Richard R. Ottley (Cambridge: CUP, 1914), 282–283; Michaël Lattke, "Die Psalmen Salomos: Orte und Intentionen," in *Die Septuaginta - Orte und Intentionen*, ed. Siegfried Kreuzer, Martin Meiser, Marcus Sigismund, WUNT 361 (Tübingen: Mohr Siebeck, 2016), 78–95; Gilles Dorival, "L'appartenance des Psaumes de Salomon au canon biblique," in *The Psalms of Solomon: Collected Essays*, ed. Felix Albrecht, Kenneth Atkinson, Patrick Pouchelle, Parabiblica 1 (Tübingen: Mohr Siebeck, 2023). On the absence of the writing from the Syriac canon, see Jean-Claude Haelewyck, "Le canon de l'Ancien Testament dans la tradition syriaque," in *L'Ancien Testament en syriaque*, ed. Françoise Briquel Chatonnet, Philippe Le Moigne, Études syriaques 5 (Paris: Geuthner : 2008), 141–171, in particular 142, note 3.

2 See the edition of Felix Albrecht, *Psalmi Salomonis*, Septuaginta. Vetus Testamentum Graecum XII.3 (Göttingen: Vandenhoeck & Ruprecht, 2018), 13–28. Similar collections exist that leave out the Psalms of Solomon, see Reinhart Ceulemans, "Did Hesychius of Jerusalem Compose an Outline of the Sapiential Books (CPG 6560[4])?" in *Philologie, herméneutique et histoire des textes entre Orient et Occident: Mélanges en hommage à Sever J. Voicu*, ed. Francesca B. Barone et al. (Turnhout: Brepols, 2017), 343–380, in particular 348.

3 The earliest quotations are from the fifteenth century, see Patrick Pouchelle, "The First Greek Quotation of the Psalms of Solomon Ever Found and its Importance for the History of the Reception of this Text," *The Psalms of Solomon: Collected Essays* (above, note 1).

The earliest printed edition of the text is that of Juan Luis de la Cerda in 1626. Swete and Rahlfs incorporated the book into their editions of the Septuagint, thus assuring it a place in recent translations and commentaries of the Septuagint corpus.[4]

In the nineteenth century, the great Julius Wellhausen devoted special attention to the Psalms of Solomon in his work on Pharisees and Sadducees.[5] In so doing, he gave an important impulse to the study of this writing. Unfortunately, he also impacted its evaluation because of his strong dislike of its contents. The equation of the authors of the songs with the Pharisees as depicted in the New Testament underlies the entire work. Even the excellent commentary of Herbert Ryle and Montague James of 1891 does not entirely shake off this prejudice.[6] A few Jewish scholars who took note of the Psalms of Solomon rectified factual mistakes, but did not find it in them to defend the work on the scholarly scene.[7] Felix Perles calls it "the least inspired and least independent work among the pseudepigrapha."[8]

The one claim to fame of the Psalms of Solomon is the messianism expressed in Sol 17. The expectation that a son of David would emerge in the near future to rule over Israel and the entire world is presupposed in the gospels, but difficult to document elsewhere. Sol 17 can with much assurance be dated to the first century BCE and establishes the existence of messianic ideas in this period. Scholarly production on Sol 17 probably exceeds that on all the other songs taken together.[9]

---

4 Albrecht, *Psalmi Salomonis*, 29–33.

5 Julius Wellhausen, *Die Pharisäer und die Sadducäer. Eine Untersuchung zur inneren jüdischen Geschichte* (Greifswald: Bamberg, 1874).

6 Herbert Ryle and Montague James, *Ψαλμοὶ Σολομῶντος. Psalms of the Pharisees, Commonly Called the Psalms of Solomon* (Cambridge: CUP, 1891).

7 See notably Felix Perles, "Zur Erklärung der Psalmen Salomos," *OLZ* 5 (1902), 269–282, 335–342, 365–372; Adolph Büchler, *Types of Jewish-Palestinian Piety from 70 B. C. E. to 70 C.E. The Ancient Pious Men* (London: Jews' College, 1922), 128–195.

8 In the original: "das gedankenarmste und auch formell das unselbständigste Werk des ganzen pseudepigraphischen Schrifttums," *OLZ* 5 (1902), 271.

9 See the critical remarks in Brad Embry, "The Psalms of Solomon and the New Testament: Intertextuality and the Need for a Re-Evaluation," *JSP* 13 (2002), 99–136.

After the discovery of new texts near the Dead Sea, studies on the Psalms of Solomon have found a new *élan*. A new awareness of the diversity of Judaism during the late Second Temple period has permitted a more differentiated approach of the text's religious background. Its stylistic peculiarities, too, can nowadays be more easily paralleled than before the publication of the Qumran texts.[10] The present work is inspired by this recent renewal of interest in the Psalms of Solomon.

## 1. The historical background of the Psalms of Solomon

Expressing their meaning, as they do, through the phraseology of scripture, the Psalms of Solomon do not clearly indicate their epoch nor their place of origin. Nevertheless, most scholars accept that the 18 songs were written in Jerusalem in the aftermath of Pompey's occupation of the city.[11] This setting indeed seems to fit the entire corpus. The songs may nonetheless have been written over several decades and by several authors, whether working successively, in parallel, or as a group. Some scholars estimate that various redactional stages can be reconstructed.[12] Only one recension is known, however,

10 See e.g. Kenneth Atkinson, *An Intertextual Study of the Psalms of Solomon* (Lewiston NY: Edwin Mellen, 2001); idem, *I Cried to the Lord: A Study of the Psalms of Solomon's Historical Background and Social Setting*, SJSJ 84 (Leiden: Brill, 2013). See also the recent collective volumes: *The Psalms of Solomon: Language, History, Theology*, ed. Eberhard Bons, Patrick Pouchelle, EJL 40 (Atlanta: SBL, 2015); *The Psalms of Solomon: Texts, Contexts, and Intertexts*, ed. G. Antony Keddie, Patrick Pouchelle, Kenneth Atkinson, EJL 54 (Atlanta: SBL Press, 2021); *The Psalms of Solomon: Collected Essays* (above, note 1)..

11 On this period, see now Nadav Sharon, *Judea under Roman Domination. The First Generation of Statelessness and Its Legacy*, EJL 46 (Atlanta: SBL, 2017).

12 Atkinson (*I Cried to the Lord*) has argued that some songs predate Pompey's conquest. See also Albrecht, *Psalmi Salomonis*, 197–235. For a redaction-critical analysis of Sol 5 only, see Hannes Bezzel, "»Und er schrieb Psalmen: dreitausendsechshundert« (11Q5, XXVII, 4f.). Psalmen-Bildung bei Ingo Baldermann im lichte von PsSal 5," in *Religion und Bildung – interdisziplinär. Festschrift für Michael Wermke zum 60. Geburtstag*, Studien zur Religiösen Bildung17 (Leipzig: Evangelische Verlagsanstalt, 2018), 25–36.

and it can fairly be said that the style and world view of the corpus remain fairly homogeneous throughout. The text of the corpus is uncertain in many passages.[13]

While time and place are reasonably certain, the writers of the Psalms of Solomon remain anonymous. Their religious background has proved difficult to define. A few articles of faith—the resurrection of the just (Sol 3:12), the affirmation of free will and divine omniscience (Sol 9:3–4)—resemble those of Rabbinic Judaism, which has led many commentators to view the authors as Pharisees.[14] Yet, as we will see, there are also some differences.[15] The resemblances may reflect the wide influence of Pharisaic thought in the first century BCE rather than the authors' adherence to a specific group.

Many modern authors discover sectarian traits, and some have tried to define the sect in question. It is true that the authors of the corpus oppose the devout of their own company to a group of sinners, who are Jews like them. But the conflict between the two groups does not seem to run along the lines of religious practice or beliefs. A frequent motif is that the sins of the opponents have been perpetrated in secret.[16] Knowing what God requires, the sinners hide their wrongdoing in the vain hope to escape punishment. This scenario suggests that the code of conduct of the two groups was the same.[17] We may note also that the Psalms of Solomon never refer to rites of accession to the assembly of the pious. The songs are the work of a distinct group, but not a closed one.

Wellhausen affirms that the Psalms of Solomon were sung in the assemblies of the devout,[18] the way Luther's hymns are sung in German churches. This seems possible in the light of passages like the following:

> **Sol 15:2–3**
> For who, O God, is strong except to confess to you in truth?
> And wherein is a person mighty except in confessing to your name?

---

13 See Albrecht, *Psalmi Salomonis*, 34–80 (with references to earlier literature).
14 See chapter 5, section 5.5.
15 See chapter 5.
16 See notably Sol 1:7; 2:17; 8:8–9.
17 See further below in chapter 2, at the end of section 2.3.
18 Wellhausen, *Pharisäer*, 113.

A new melody with an ode in gladness of heart,
the fruit of the lips with the tuned instrument of the tongue,
the first fruit of the lips from a devout and righteous heart.[19]

Whether all the songs were meant to be performed in worship, and whether this was their original purpose is hard to say. Certainly they are liturgical. Many of them address God directly or call upon God in the third person. They are also communal, they presuppose a collective of like-minded Jews for whom religious practices were an important part of their lives. Numerous passages are formulated in the first person plural. And they are educational, guiding their addressees in the correct interpretation of both scripture and contemporary events, while at the same time modeling exemplary behavior in times of crisis.[20]

## 2. The present study

As was hinted at above, the Psalms of Solomon express most of what they have to say in words and phrases lifted from earlier writings. The authors tend to clothe their thoughts in language borrowed from the Pentateuch, Prophets, Psalms, and other writings. The Psalms of Solomon are like a collage. New meanings are expressed through the combination of phrases "cut and pasted" from other texts. This stylistic peculiarity is rooted in a long habit of reading the texts in question, but there is more to it than mere familiarity. The density of intertextual connections suggests that, to the authors, scriptural language is the uniquely appropriate way to express religious meaning.[21] They see themselves as successors to the authors of old, Moses, the Prophets and, in particular, David.

While the anthological style of Psalms of Solomon is indeed striking, particularly when the Psalms are compared to their "canonical" namesakes, it is at the same time a well-known feature of contemporary compositions. Some of the hymns imbricated in Hellenistic-Jewish writings, such as the Song of Azariah in Dan 3, exhibit the same

19 See also Sol 3:1–2.
20 See e.g. Rodney A. Werline, "The Formation of the Pious Person in the Psalms of Solomon," in *The Psalms of Solomon: Language, History, Theology* (above, n. 8), 133–154.
21 See further in chapter 2.

combination of dependence on scriptural diction with daring freedom in expressing new ideas.[22] One could also name some passages in the New Testament, such as the songs in the first part of the Gospel of Luke. Among Hebrew writings, the Hymns Scroll from Qumran provides excellent material for comparison.[23] Although each writing needs to be studied in its own right, there is definitely a family relationship among these writings that speaks to the more general cultural and religious climate of the time.

The dynamics of the Psalms of Solomon's use of scripture are fascinating and will be further explored in chapter 2. But the principal objective of the present monograph lies elsewhere. The inquiry will focus on the nature of the scriptural text, or texts, available to the authors. Can their text be located geographically? Does it occupy a specific place in the textual history of the writings referred to? Is it possible to situate it in relation to known recensions or textual forms of scripture, from the same period or from other periods?

Surprisingly, the answer to some of these questions is yes. A crucial step is to determine the original language of the allusions. Venturing out from there, it will indeed be possible to define several important features of the scriptural text underlying the Psalms of Solomon (chapters 3 and 4).

The text-historical conclusions open up new perspectives in the study of the text and the group that produced it (chapter 5).

One methodological and one terminological remark will round off this brief introduction. Textual data culled from an ancient text attested only in late manuscripts and about whose origins and setting in life little is known are often somewhat uncertain. Any individual passage is susceptible to various interpretations. For this reason, I will seek to build my case on patterns rather than single examples. When a series of examples exhibit a notable tendency, the cumulative argument can be compelling.

---

22 See Jan Joosten, "The Prayer of Azariah (DanLXX 3): Sources and Origin," in *Septuagint and Reception*, ed. Johann Cook, VTS 127 (Leiden: Brill, 2009), 5–16.

23 See e.g. Julie Hughes, *Scriptural Allusions and Exegesis in the Hodayot*, STDJ 59 (Leiden: Brill, 2006).

As to terminology, the earlier writings that resound in the Psalms of Solomon on every page were dear to their authors and spoke to them with authority. Thus it seems legitimate to refer to them with the term "scripture." The authors regarded the books they referred to as scripture. The term is not meant to militate for a specific view on the history of the canon or the textual stability of the writings in question. For stylistic reasons, I will sometimes use the term "biblical" to refer to the same writings. This term is anachronistic, because when the Psalms of Solomon were written, the Bible did not yet exist, but it is still a useful one. It so happens that most of the intertexts of the Psalms of Solomon later ended up in the so-called Jewish (or Rabbinic) canon and thus also in the various Christian Bibles.

# 1.
# Defining Criteria and Collecting a Database

Many passages in the Psalms of Solomon are redolent of scripture.[1] Because of their date, after 63 BCE, this phenomenon can only be interpreted in terms of influence from the biblical texts on the Psalms of Solomon. Unless they can be explained from accident, similarities in language and thought indicate dependence. The author or authors of the Psalms of Solomon knew many writings that are today part of the Hebrew Bible and venerated them. Consequently, in their religious poetry they reused themes and expressions from those writings, developing them and interpreting them in various ways.

In the present chapter, allusions to scripture in the Psalms of Solomon will be listed and briefly discussed. Allusions are defined as cases where the author is wittingly drawing on the language of a specific passage in earlier writings.[2] The objective has been to include

1 As will be detailed at the end of this chapter, the writings alluded to in the Psalms of Solomon include the five books of the Pentateuch, all the Latter Prophets (if we consider the Twelve a single book), Psalms and Proverbs. It is impossible to say whether the authors conceived of these writings as belonging to various subcollections, or attributed different degrees of authority to them. There are no certain allusions to writings that did not end up in the Rabbinic canon. Note, however, that Sol 11 possibly draws on Baruch 4:36–5:8 (though it may be the reverse); the connection is to be discussed in the Appendix.

2 Some allusions only reflect the thought of a scriptural passage but not the language (compare e.g. Sol 17:33a with Deut 17:16). Such examples are useless for text-historical analysis and have not been included in this study. Other allusions refer to a larger section of scripture (e.g. Sol 14:3 and Gen 2–3, the "garden of Eden"; Sol 17:19 and Gen 6–7, the flood story). Again, these have not been included.

only relatively certain examples. Diagnostic features allowing us to identify such cases include the following:[3]

1) Where a passage in scripture and a specific passage in Psalms of Solomon share a striking combination of words, or
2) where they share a striking combination of one or more words with a literary or religious motif, an allusion is likely.[4]
3) The use of a quotation formula also suggests the presence of a reference to scripture.[5]

Even with these criteria, the identification of scriptural language involves some subjectivity. Fortunately, there are many cases. If one or two examples were found to be dubious, the tendencies of intertextual connection would still be clear. Readers who consider three or four times the amount of cases should have been included may be satisfied that the present study is based on a representative sample.[6]

As is to be expected for a Greek document, many scriptural references in the Psalms of Solomon resonate with the Septuagint specifically. Nevertheless, to keep an open mind, we will include the Hebrew version of passages referred to, according to the MT, alongside the Greek version. The comparative relevance of the different texts will be evaluated in chapters 3 and 4.

---

3 For more extensive exploration of criteria allowing the identification of allusions, see Armin Lange, Matthias Weigold, *Biblical Quotations and Allusions in Second Temple Jewish Literature* (Göttingen: Vandenhoeck & Ruprecht, 2011), 23–34.

4 In some instances, it is hard to pinpoint the reference of the allusion because the wording is found in several passages. Kim has argued that Sol 2:16, 34; 17:8 allude to Ps 62/61:13, see Kyoung-Shik Kim, *God Will Judge Each One According to Works (Judgment According to Works and Psalm 62 in Early Judaism and the New Testament* (Berlin: De Gruyter, 2010), 112—113. The claim is possible, but it is possible also that the intertext is Prov 24:12 or Lam 3:64. Or perhaps the phrase "to repay so and so for their work" became a popular expression not associated with any specific passage.

5 The only instance of a quotation formula is found in Sol 9:2.

6 The commentaries refer to many possible intertexts that do not satisfy our criteria and have not been included. Atkinson's monograph, too, is rather maximalistic. A very useful resource in putting together the present list has been Lange, Weigold, *Biblical Quotations and* Allusions, in particular 246–247.

In the present chapter, terms such as "allusion," "reference" and "intertextual connection" will be used more or less promiscuously. A more differentiated analysis of the reuse of scripture in Psalms of Solomon will be offered in chapter 2.

## 1.1. List of allusions

Sol 1:3
ἐλογισάμην ἐν καρδίᾳ μου ὅτι ἐπλήσθην δικαιοσύνης
ἐν τῷ εὐθηνῆσαί με καὶ **πολλὴν** γενέσθαι **ἐν τέκνοις**.
I thought in my heart that I was full of righteousness,
when I prospered and had become rich in children[7]

1 Sam/1 Kgds 2:5
καὶ ἡ **πολλὴ ἐν τέκνοις** ἠσθένησεν
and she who is rich in children became weak
וְרַבַּת בָּנִים אֻמְלָלָה
but she who has many children is forlorn[8]

The use of the expression "rich in children" can with confidence be said to be borrowed from the earlier text. The Greek expression πολλὴ ἐν τέκνοις is found only in Sol 1:3 and in the song of Hannah (1 Kgds 2:5; Ode 3:5).[9]

The Greek idiom πολὺς ἐν "great, or numerous, in regard to" is found four more times in the Septuagint, but does not seem to be otherwise attested in ancient Greek.[10] The rareness of the grammatical construction enhances the likelihood of a link between our two passages.

7 All English translations of Septuagintal texts, including the Psalms of Solomon, follow the New English Translation of the Septuagint (NETS), unless indicated otherwise.
8 Translations of the Hebrew Bible follow the NRSV, unless indicated otherwise.
9 We need to bear in mind that the Song of Hannah was a very famous text in antiquity. Note that 1 Kgds 2:5 is quoted twice by Philo (*Deus* 10; *Mut* 143), who otherwise quotes rather little from Jewish writings other than the Pentateuch.
10 See Deut 33:6 πολὺς ἐν ἀριθμῷ; Prov 14:29 πολὺς ἐν φρονήσει; Job 11:3 πολὺς ἐν ῥήμασιν (quoted in 1 Clem 30:5); Ezek 22:5 πολλὴ ἐν ταῖς ἀνομίαις.

**Sol 2:8**
**ἀπέστρεψεν** γὰρ **τὸ πρόσωπον αὐτοῦ ἀπὸ ἐλέους** αὐτῶν
He turned away his face from pitying them

Isa 59:2
καὶ διὰ τὰς ἁμαρτίας ὑμῶν **ἀπέστρεψεν τὸ πρόσωπον αὐτοῦ ἀφ'** ὑμῶν τοῦ μὴ **ἐλεῆσαι.**
and because of your sins he has turned his face away from you so as not to show mercy

וְחַטֹּאותֵיכֶם הִסְתִּירוּ פָנִים מִכֶּם מִשְּׁמוֹעַ
and your sins have hidden his face from you so that he does not hear

Although the action of pitying is expressed by a noun in the Psalms of Solomon and a verbal phrase in Isaiah, the wording and the thought are sufficiently close to identify the allusion. Note that the Hebrew text of Isa 59:2 has the people's sin as the subject of the verb, and refers to "hearing" and not to "pitying" explicitly.

**Sol 2:12**
**ἀπέναντι τοῦ ἡλίου παρεδειγμάτισαν** ἀδικίας αὐτῶν.
Before the sun they (the Romans) paraded their (the Jerusalemites') injustices

Num 25:4
καὶ **παραδειγμάτισον** αὐτοὺς κυρίῳ **ἀπέναντι τοῦ ἡλίου**
and make an example of them (the leaders of the people) to the Lord before the sun

וְהוֹקַע אוֹתָם לַיהוָה נֶגֶד הַשָּׁמֶשׁ
and impale them in the sun before the LORD

The verb παραδειγματίζω "to make a show of" is referred to the sins in the first passage, to the sinners in the second. In spite of this difference in usage, there can be no doubt that Sol 2:12 draws on the wording of the verse in Numbers. The verb occurs 8 times in the Septuagint, but only in these two passages does it combine with ἀπέναντι τοῦ ἡλίου.

**Sol 2:17**
**ἐξήλειψας τὸ μνημόσυνον** αὐτῶν ἀπὸ τῆς γῆς
you have wiped out their (the sinners') memorial from the earth

Exod 17:14
Αλοιφῇ **ἐξαλείψω τὸ μνημόσυνον** Αμαληκ ἐκ τῆς ὑπὸ τὸν οὐρανόν

With a wipe out I will wipe out the memorial of Amalek from beneath heaven.

מָחֹה אֶמְחֶה אֶת־זֵכֶר עֲמָלֵק מִתַּחַת הַשָּׁמָיִם׃

I will utterly blot out the remembrance of Amalek from under heaven

The expression ἐξαλείφω τὸ μνημόσυνον, "to wipe out the memorial," is unless I err found only in these two passages.[11]

**Sol 2:18**

**ὁ θεὸς κριτὴς δίκαιος** καὶ οὐ θαυμάσει πρόσωπον

God is a righteous judge, and he will not marvel at a person

Psalm 7:12

**ὁ θεὸς κριτὴς δίκαιος** καὶ ἰσχυρὸς καὶ μακρόθυμος

God is a righteous judge, and strong and patient

אֱלֹהִים שׁוֹפֵט צַדִּיק

God is a righteous judge

The notion that God is righteous in his judgments is found throughout the Psalms of Solomon.[12] In Sol 2:18 it is expressed with a phrase taken from Psalms. The precise clause is attested only here in the Septuagint.

**Sol 2:20**

**περιεζώσατο σάκκον** ἀντὶ ἐνδύματος εὐπρεπείας,
**σχοινίον** περὶ **τὴν κεφαλὴν** αὐτῆς ἀντὶ στεφάνου
She put on sackcloth instead of beautiful clothing,
a rope around her head instead of a crown

1 Kgs 20/3 Kgds 21:32 (1 Kgs 20/3 Kgds 21:31)

καὶ **περιεζώσαντο σάκκους** ἐπὶ τὰς ὀσφύας αὐτῶν
καὶ ἔθεσαν **σχοινία** ἐπὶ τὰς **κεφαλὰς** αὐτῶν
And they tied sackcloths around their waists
and put ropes on their heads

וַיַּחְגְּרוּ שַׂקִּים בְּמׇתְנֵיהֶם וַחֲבָלִים בְּרָאשֵׁיהֶם

So they tied sackcloth around their waists, put ropes on their heads

11 Note that the Deuteronomic parallel in Deut 25:19 uses ὄνομα "name" instead μνημόσυνον. With ὄνομα the expression is more frequent (see e.g. Deut 29:19; Psalm 9:6).

12 See e.g. Sol 2:10, 15; 3:3; 4:8; 5:1; 8:7, 8, 23, 25; 9:5; 10:5.

Although rope and sackcloth are mentioned together in other passages,[13] having the rope on the head is attested only in these. This makes the allusion nearly certain. The different preposition in the second clause (περί versus ἐπί) is to be explained as an adaptation to Greek idiom in Sol 2:20.[14]

**Sol 3:2**
ψάλλε καὶ γρηγόρησον ἐπὶ τὴν γρηγόρησιν αὐτοῦ,
**ὅτι ἀγαθὸς ψαλμὸς τῷ θεῷ** ἐξ ἀγαθῆς καρδίας.
Play, and be fully awake in wakefulness for him,
for a good melody to God is from a good heart

Psalm 147/146:1
Αἰνεῖτε τὸν κύριον, **ὅτι ἀγαθὸν ψαλμός· τῷ θεῷ** ἡμῶν ἡδυνθείη αἴνεσις
Praise the Lord, because a melody is a good thing, to our God may praise be pleasing.
הַלְלוּ יָהּ כִּי־טוֹב זַמְּרָה אֱלֹהֵינוּ כִּי־נָעִים נָאוָה תְהִלָּה

Although the thought expressed in these two passages may not be exactly the same, the presence of five identical words in sequence can hardly be due to chance. According to the texts cited from the standard editions, the grammar diverges. However, nothing would have prevented an ancient reader from taking τῷ θεῷ ἡμῶν in Psalm 147/146:1 with what preceded, and this seems to be what the author of Sol 3 has done. Moreover, several important manuscripts read ἀγαθός in Ps 147/146:1 instead of ἀγαθόν as adopted in the critical edition, and it may well be that the masculine figured in the text known to the author of Sol 3.

**Sol 3:4**
οὐκ **ὀλιγωρήσει** δίκαιος **παιδευόμενος** ὑπὸ **κυρίου**
The righteous does not despise being disciplined by the Lord

Prov 3:11
Υἱέ, μὴ **ὀλιγώρει παιδείας κυρίου**
My son, do not belittle the Lord's discipline
מוּסַר יְהוָה בְּנִי אַל־תִּמְאָס
My child, do not despise the LORD's discipline

---

13 See e.g. Isa 3:24; Joseph and Aseneth 13:3; 14:16.

14 Note that Josephus does something similar in his paraphrase of the same story in *Antiquities* 8:385, σχοινία ταῖς κεφαλαῖς περιθέμενοι, "with ropes *about* their heads."

The verb ὀλιγωρέω is not a frequent one and these are the only attestations of it in the Septuagint.[15] The combination of the verb with the notion of divine education leaves little doubt about the intertextual connection. We should note, however, that the grammar is different: in Proverbs the verb governs an object in the genitive, while in Sol the verb is used absolutely. Both usages are well attested in the classical language.

**Sol 3:8**
**ἐξιλάσατο περὶ ἀγνοίας** ἐν νηστείᾳ καὶ ταπεινώσει ψυχῆς αὐτοῦ
(the righteous) made atonement for sins of ignorance by fasting and humiliation of his soul

Lev 5:18
καὶ **ἐξιλάσεται** περὶ αὐτοῦ ὁ ἱερεὺς **περὶ** τῆς **ἀγνοίας** αὐτοῦ
and the priest shall make atonement for him concerning his ignorance
וְכִפֶּר עָלָיו הַכֹּהֵן עַל שִׁגְגָתוֹ
and the priest shall make atonement on his behalf for his error

The verb ἐξιλάσκομαι "to make atonement" is a frequent one in the Septuagint, and it is rather often constructed with περί to designate either the sin or the persons on whose behalf atonement is made. The noun ἀγνοία "ignorance, unwitting sin" is less well represented but it is far from rare. Nevertheless, these two are the only verses which combine ἐξιλάσκομαι περί with ἀγνοία.[16]

**Sol 3:10**
**προσέθηκεν ἁμαρτίας ἐφ' ἁμαρτίας** τῇ ζωῇ αὐτοῦ
He has added sin upon sin in his lifetime

Isa 30:1
προσθεῖναι ἁμαρτίας ἐφ' ἁμαρτίαις
to add sins to sins
לְמַעַן סְפוֹת חַטָּאת עַל־חַטָּאת

15 Albrecht, *Psalmi Salomonis*, 182.

16 Note however 1 Esd 9:20 (cf. Ezr 10:19) εἰς **ἐξιλασμὸν** κριοὺς ὑπὲρ τῆς **ἀγνοίας** αὐτῶν "as expiation to offer rams for their mistake"; but the free rendering in 1 Esd would itself seem to be dependent on Lev 5:18.

The notion of adding sin to sin recurs surprisingly often in biblical and parabiblical literature.[17] The precise formulation is exclusive to these two passages, however, and can hardly be due to chance.

> Sol 3:12
> οἱ δὲ φοβούμενοι τὸν κύριον **ἀναστήσονται εἰς ζωὴν αἰώνιον**
> but those who fear the Lord shall rise to everlasting life

> Dan 12:2
> LXX καὶ πολλοὶ τῶν καθευδόντων ἐν τῷ πλάτει τῆς γῆς **ἀναστήσονται**, οἱ μὲν **εἰς ζωὴν αἰώνιον**, οἱ δὲ εἰς ὀνειδισμόν οἱ δὲ εἰς διασπορὰν καὶ αἰσχύνην αἰώνιον.
> And many of those who sleep in the flat of the earth will arise, some to everlasting life but others to shame and others to dispersion [and contempt] everlasting.
> Θ′ καὶ πολλοὶ τῶν καθευδόντων ἐν γῆς χώματι ἐξεγερθήσονται, οὗτοι εἰς ζωὴν αἰώνιον καὶ οὗτοι εἰς ὀνειδισμὸν καὶ εἰς αἰσχύνην αἰώνιον
> And many of those who sleep in a mound of earth will be awakened, these to everlasting life and those to shame and everlasting contempt.
> וְרַבִּים מִיְּשֵׁנֵי אַדְמַת־עָפָר יָקִיצוּ אֵלֶּה לְחַיֵּי עוֹלָם וְאֵלֶּה לַחֲרָפוֹת לְדִרְאוֹן עוֹלָם
> Many of those who sleep in the dust of the earth shall awake, some to everlasting life, and some to shame and everlasting contempt.

The verb ἀνίστημι is used for rising from the dead elsewhere in the Septuagint.[18] And "eternal life" is a much-discussed topic in the first century BCE.[19] However, the precise phrase, "to rise to eternal life," is otherwise found only in the Old Greek of Dan 12:2. This makes an intertextual link very likely.

Note that the similarity to the version that goes under the name of Theodotion is less impressive.

> Sol 4:3
> καὶ **ἡ χεὶρ** αὐτοῦ **ἐν πρώτοις ἐπ' αὐτὸν** ὡς ἐν ζήλει

17 The original source text may be Deut 29:18 (where the Septuagint follows a different interpretation). See also Sir 3:27; 5:5; Sol 3:6.

18 See Takamitsu Muraoka, *A Greek-English Lexicon of the Septuagint* (Leuven: Peeters, 2009), 54.

19 See e.g. 2 Mac 7:9; Sol 13:11; 14:3; CD 3:20; 1QS 4:7; the Greek phrase ζωὴ αἰώνιος is rare before the NT, but see 1 Enoch 10:10.

And his hand is the first upon him as if in zeal

Deut 17:7

καὶ **ἡ χεὶρ** τῶν μαρτύρων ἔσται **ἐπ' αὐτῷ ἐν πρώτοις** θανατῶσαι αὐτόν

And the hand of the witnesses shall be the first against him to put him to death.

יַד הָעֵדִים תִּהְיֶה־בּוֹ בָרִאשֹׁנָה לַהֲמִיתוֹ

The hand of the witnesses shall be the first against him to put him to death.

A close parallel to Deut 17:7 is relevant as well: Deut 13:10, αἱ χεῖρές σου ἔσονται ἐπ' αὐτὸν ἐν πρώτοις, "Your own hands shall be first against him to kill him." While "the hand of X is against Y" is a common expression in the Bible, and ἐν πρώτοις is a regular way of expressing "first," the combination of the two is found only in these three texts. The minor divergence between ἐπί + dative versus ἐπί + accusative does not put an obstacle in the way of this view. In the expression "the hand of X is against Y," the use of the accusative is far more common than the dative.[20]

The idea too, that the hand of the one accusing a sinner is the one to "throw the first stone" clearly draws on the Deuteronomic passages.

**Sol 4:19**

**Σκορπισθείησαν** σάρκες **ἀνθρωπαρέσκων** ὑπὸ θηρίων,
καὶ **ὀστᾶ** παρανόμων κατέναντι τοῦ ἡλίου ἐν ἀτιμίᾳ

May the flesh of the men-pleasers be scattered by wild beasts, and may the bones of the transgressors of the law lie before the sun in dishonor

Psalm 53/52:6

ὁ θεὸς **διεσκόρπισεν ὀστᾶ ἀνθρωπαρέσκων**

God scattered bones of men-pleasers

אֱלֹהִים פִּזַּר עַצְמוֹת חֹנָךְ

God will scatter the bones of one who encamps against you

The noun ἀνθρωπάρεσκος "pleaser of humans" is found once in the Septuagint version of Psalm 53/52:6 and three times in the Psalms of Solomon (Sol 4:7, 8, 19). It is not attested in secular writings and

20 The dative is found only in Deut 2:15; 17:7 (with variant readings with ἐπί + accusative in both passages). For the accusative, see, in addition to Deut 13:10, Gen 16:12; 37:27; Ezra 7:6.

may in fact be a neologism created by the translator of the Psalms.[21] The combination with the verb σκορπίζω/διασκορπίζω "to scatter" makes an intertextual connection virtually certain, and the presence of ὀστᾶ "bones" in both texts further confirms the case. The allusion is nevertheless a free one in which the later author draws on the earlier text without reproducing it literally.

**Sol 4:20**
**ὀφθαλμοὺς ἐκκόψαισαν κόρακες** ὑποκρινομένων
May ravens peck out the eyes of hypocrites

Prov 30:17
**ὀφθαλμὸν** καταγελῶντα πατρὸς καὶ ἀτιμάζοντα γῆρας μητρός,
**ἐκκόψαισαν** αὐτὸν **κόρακες** ἐκ τῶν φαράγγων
An eye that derides a father and scorns the old age of a mother,
May ravens from the ravines peck it out
עַ֤יִן ׀ תִּֽלְעַ֣ג לְאָב֮ וְתָב֪וּז לִֽיקֲּהַ֫ת־אֵ֥ם יִקְּר֣וּהָ עֹרְבֵי־נַ֑חַל
The eye that mocks a father and scorns to obey a mother,
may ravens of the valley peck it out

Three words from the picturesque curse in Prov 30:17 are taken over in Sol 4:20, making it certain that the author is thinking of the earlier passage.[22] The verb is in the same mood, but there is a variation in the number of the noun ὀφθαλμός.

**Sol 5:2**
ἐν τῷ **κεκραγέναι** με πρὸς σὲ **μὴ παρασιωπήσῃς ἀπ᾽ ἐμοῦ**
when I cry out to you, do not pass me by in silence

Psalm 28/27:1
Πρὸς σέ, κύριε, **ἐκέκραξα**, ὁ θεός μου, **μὴ παρασιωπήσῃς ἀπ᾽ ἐμοῦ**
To you, O Lord, I cried, my God, do not pass me by in silence
אֵלֶ֤יךָ יְהוָ֨ה ׀ אֶקְרָא֮ צוּרִ֢י אַֽל־תֶּחֱרַ֫שׁ מִ֥מֶּנִּי
To you, O LORD, I call; my rock, do not refuse to hear me

---

21 On the Greek word and on its possible Hebrew equivalent, see Patrick Pouchelle, "ἀνθρωπάρεσκος," in *Historical and Theological Lexicon of the Septuagint*, ed. Eberhard Bons (Tübingen: Mohr Siebeck, 2020), 737–744.

22 The expression ἐκκόπτω ὀφθαλμούς "to peck out the eyes" is found also in Num 16:14.

The combination of the verb κράζω "to cry out" with the Hebraizing expression παρασιωπάω ἀπό "to turn a deaf ear to" indicates literary dependence.[23]

**Sol 5:3**
οὐ γὰρ **λήψεταί τις σκῦλα παρὰ** ἀνδρὸς δυνατοῦ[24]
For no one will take booty from a strong man.

Isa 49:24
μὴ **λήμψεταί τις παρὰ** γίγαντος **σκῦλα**
Shall one take booty from a giant?

הֲיֻקַּח מִגִּבּוֹר מַלְקוֹחַ
Shall booty be taken from a strong man?

Although the application of the parable appears to differ in these passages, the parable itself is the same, and the amount of words common to both makes literary borrowing likely.

In Sol 5:3, "from a strong man" is arguably closer to the Hebrew than to the Septuagint. While this is probably not a chance agreement, it does not necessarily indicate direct dependence on a Hebrew text. Further discussion on this point will be forthcoming in chapter 4.

**Sol 5:5**
**Ἐν τῷ θλίβεσθαι** ἡμᾶς **ἐπικαλεσόμεθά** σε εἰς βοήθειαν,
When we are distressed we will call upon you for help

**Sol 15:1**
**Ἐν τῷ θλίβεσθαί με ἐπεκαλεσάμην** τὸ ὄνομα **κυρίου**,
When I was in distress, I called upon the name of the Lord

Psalm 18/17:7[25]
καὶ **ἐν τῷ θλίβεσθαί με ἐπεκαλεσάμην** τὸν **κύριον**
And when I was being afflicted, I called upon the Lord

---

23 Albrecht, *Psalmi Salomonis*, 182. The expression παρασιωπάω ἀπό is found also in 1 Kgds 7:8.

24 Instead of οὐ γὰρ λήψεταί τις σκῦλα, in which τίς is based on a conjecture, Albrecht edits the text of 260: οὐ γὰρ λήψεταί σκῦλα ἄνθρωπος. 260 has the support of the Syriac version, but it is not easy to explain how ἄνθρωπος came to be omitted from the other witnesses. For the question at hand the variant reading makes little difference. Note that in Isa 49:24, τίς is omitted in one minuscule, showing that such an omission could happen by accident.

25 Note also the parallel in 2 Kgds 22:7 ἐν τῷ θλίβεσθαί με ἐπικαλέσομαι κύριον, with the verb in the future tense.

בַּצַּר־לִי אֶקְרָא יְהוָה
In my distress I called upon the Lord

The wording and the thought in these passages are so close as to make a direct link between them a near certainty.

**Sol 5:12**
τίς **χρηστὸς καὶ ἐπιεικὴς** ἀλλ᾽ ἢ **σύ**
Who is kind and forgiving but you?

Psal 86/85:5
ὅτι **σύ**, κύριε, **χρηστὸς καὶ ἐπιεικής**
Because it is you, O Lord, who are kind and gentle
כִּי־אַתָּה אֲדֹנָי טוֹב וְסַלָּח
For you, O Lord, are good and forgiving

The phrase "kind and gentle" is not found elsewhere in the Septuagint.[26]

**Sol 5:19**
**εὐλογημένη ἡ δόξα κυρίου**, ὅτι αὐτὸς βασιλεὺς ἡμῶν
Blessed is the glory of the Lord, for he is our king

Ezek 3:12
**Εὐλογημένη ἡ δόξα κυρίου** ἐκ τοῦ τόπου αὐτοῦ
Blessed is the glory of the Lord from his place
בָּרוּךְ כְּבוֹד־יְהוָה מִמְּקוֹמוֹ
Blessed is the Glory of the Lord from his place[27]

The phrase "blessed is the glory of the Lord" is found only in these two passages, making an intertextual connection nearly certain.[28]

**Sol 7:3**
σὺ **ἐν θελήματί** σου **παίδευσον** ἡμᾶς
Discipline us by your will

Hos 10:10
ἦλθεν παιδεῦσαι αὐτούς,
he has come to educate them.

26 The cultural background of the phrase is in Hellenistic formulas addressed to the king, see e.g. *Aristeas* 290.

27 The NRSV translates: "as the glory of the LORD rose from its place." This is based on a conjectural reading, ברום, instead of ברוך, see BHS. The Septuagint concurs with the Masoretic text.

28 Note, however, that the thought is paralleled in the Septuagint of Isa 64:10 ἡ δόξα, ἣν ηὐλόγησαν οἱ πατέρες ἡμῶν, "the glory that our fathers blessed."

בְּאַוָּתִי וְאֶסֳּרֵם
It is in my desire that I should chastise them (KJV)

Although the meaning of the Hebrew text of Hos 10:10 is perhaps not as clear as one should wish, the KJV indicates that it could easily be given a meaning strikingly similar to that of Sol 7:3.[29] The close association of God's will and his discipline or education makes a literary connection between the two passages likely.

The textual form of Sol 7:3 diverges from the Septuagint. The source of the allusion may be the Hebrew text, or a non-Septuagintal Greek version (see chapter 4).

**Sol 7:6**
Ἐν τῷ **κατασκηνοῦν τὸ ὄνομά** σου **ἐν μέσῳ** ἡμῶν ἐλεηθησόμεθα
While your name dwells in our midst, we shall find pity

Ezek 43:7
Εώρακας, υἱὲ ἀνθρώπου, τὸν τόπον τοῦ θρόνου μου καὶ τὸν τόπον τοῦ ἴχνους τῶν ποδῶν μου, ἐν οἷς **κατασκηνώσει τὸ ὄνομά μου ἐν μέσῳ** οἴκου Ισραηλ τὸν αἰῶνα
You have seen; son of man, the place of my throne and the place of the print of my feet, in which my name shall encamp in the midst of the house of Israel forever
בֶּן־אָדָם אֶת־מְקוֹם כִּסְאִי וְאֶת־מְקוֹם כַּפּוֹת רַגְלַי אֲשֶׁר אֶשְׁכָּן־שָׁם בְּתוֹךְ בְּנֵי־יִשְׂרָאֵל לְעוֹלָם
Mortal, this is the place of my throne and the place for the soles of my feet, where I will reside among the people of Israel forever.

The formula stating that "God's name dwells" in a certain place is surprisingly rare in the Septuagint.[30] The combination of this formula with the prepositional phrase "in the midst of" is found only in these two passages. Note that the textual correspondence in this case is with the Septuagint version only while the MT expresses a different meaning.

**Sol 8:2**
**ὡς καταιγὶς** πυρὸς πολλοῦ φερομένου **δι᾽ ἐρήμου**

29 See also the Vulgate: *iuxta desiderium meum corripiam eos* "according to my desire I will chastise them." The Vulgate may here reflect a lost reading of Aquila or Symmachus.

30 See Jer 7:13; Ezra 6:12; Neh 1:9. In the Hebrew text, the phrase is frequent, but it is usually translated differently in the Septuagint.

like a hurricane with mighty fire sweeping through the wilderness

Isa 21:1
**ὡς καταιγὶς δι᾽ ἐρήμου** διέλθοι
As a whirlwind might pass through a wilderness
כְּסוּפוֹת בַּנֶּגֶב לַחֲלֹף
As whirlwinds in the Negeb sweep on

Neither καταιγίς nor ἔρημος are rare words in the Septuagint. Nevertheless, they are combined in an original simile in these two verses, making an intertextual connection likely.

**Sol 8:9**
υἱὸς μετὰ μητρὸς καὶ πατὴρ μετὰ θυγατρὸς **συνεφύροντο**
they committed incest, son with mother and father with daughter

Ezek 22:6
ἰδοὺ οἱ ἀφηγούμενοι οἴκου Ισραηλ ἕκαστος πρὸς τοὺς συγγενεῖς αὐτοῦ **συνανεφύροντο** ἐν σοί
Behold, the leaders of the house of Israel, each with his kindred, they wallowed together in you.
הִנֵּה נְשִׂיאֵי יִשְׂרָאֵל אִישׁ לִזְרֹעוֹ הָיוּ בָךְ
The princes of Israel in you, everyone according to his power, have been bent on shedding blood

The claim of intertextuality in this case rests on the combination of a rare word and a striking motif.[31] The verb συμφύρω means "to knead together," "to mix, to mingle," and is used in sexual contexts in both the Septuagint and Greek literature.[32] As the NETS translation of Sol 8:9 brings out correctly, the verse speaks of incest. The same is almost certainly the case in the Septuagint version of Ezek 22:6. Note that the

31 See in more detail, Jan Joosten, "The Accusation of Incest in Psalms of Solomon 8:9. Apologetics, Halakha, and Exegesis," in *Tempel, Lehrhaus, Synagoge. Orte jüdischen Lernens und Lebens. Festschrift für Wolfgang Kraus*, ed. Christian Eberhart et al. (Paderborn: Ferdinand Schöningh, 2020), 205–215.

32 In the Septuagint, note particularly Hos 4:14, μετὰ τῶν πορνῶν συνεφύροντο, they "were associating with whores." Note also Jer 3:2, where the cognate ἐκφύρω is used to render Hebrew שגל "to rape, to violate."

Hebrew text, at least according to the Tiberian vocalization does not address incest.

Although the question of incest is not skirted in the Hebrew Bible, it is evoked only rarely.[33] The combination of verb and motif strongly suggests that the author of Sol 8 was thinking of the earlier passage as he composed his text.

In their editions of Ezekiel, both Ziegler and Rahlfs print the reading of the Codex Alexandrinus, συνανεφύροντο. However, the reading συνεφύροντο, the exact same form as in Sol 8:9, is well attested for Ezek 22:6, being found in Pap. 967, the codex Vaticanus, and many minuscules in the *O* and *L* groups. In light of this attestation, συνεφύροντο may well be the older reading. But even if it is not, it may be the form of the text the author of Sol 8 knew.

**Sol 8:14a**
Διὰ τοῦτο **ἐκέρασεν αὐτοῖς** ὁ θεὸς **πνεῦμα πλανήσεως**
Therefore God mixed for them a spirit of confusion;

Isa 19:14
κύριος γὰρ **ἐκέρασεν αὐτοῖς πνεῦμα πλανήσεως**
For the Lord has prepared for them a spirit of error
יְהוָה מָסַךְ בְּקִרְבָּהּ רוּחַ עִוְעִים
The LORD has poured into them a spirit of confusion

The author of Sol 8 lifted a sequence of four words from the text of Isaiah. Note that κεράννυμι "to mix" is attested with πνεῦμα as direct object only in these two passages.

**Sol 8:14b**
**ἐπότισεν** αὐτοὺς **ποτήριον οἴνου ἀκράτου** εἰς μέθην.
He gave them a cup of undiluted wine to drink, that they might become drunk.

Jer 25/32:15
Λαβὲ τὸ **ποτήριον** τοῦ **οἴνου** τοῦ **ἀκράτου** τούτου ἐκ χειρός μου καὶ **ποτιεῖς** πάντα τὰ ἔθνη
Take from my hand this cup of this unmixed wine, and you shall make all the nations, to them to whom I send you, drink
קַח אֶת־כּוֹס הַיַּיִן הַחֵמָה הַזֹּאת מִיָּדִי וְהִשְׁקִיתָה אֹתוֹ אֶת־כָּל־הַגּוֹיִם
Take from my hand this cup of the wine of wrath, and make all the nations to whom I send you drink it

33 See Gen 19; Lev 18 and 20; 2 Sam 14.

Although the motif of the cup, figuring God's wrath, is a frequent one in the Bible, these two verses are the only ones that share the four words highlighted in the quotations.[34] Note that the Hebrew text speaks of "wine of wrath" while the Septuagint and Sol 8:14 agree in speaking of "unmixed wine."

**Sol 9:2**
ἐν παντὶ ἔθνει **ἡ διασπορὰ** τοῦ Ισραηλ κατὰ τὸ ῥῆμα τοῦ θεοῦ
Among every nation is Israel's dispersion, according to the word of God.

Deut 28:25
καὶ ἔσῃ ἐν **διασπορᾷ** ἐν πάσαις ταῖς βασιλείαις τῆς γῆς
And you shall be in dispersion in all the kingdoms of the earth.
וְהָיִיתָ לְזַעֲוָה לְכֹל מַמְלְכוֹת הָאָרֶץ
You shall become an object of horror to all the kingdoms of the earth.

The two verses have only one word in common. Nevertheless, a good case can be made for a connection, for the thought of the two passages is nearly identical.

Moreover, this is arguably the one case in the Psalms of Solomon where a reference to scripture is explicitly indicated. If "according to the word of God" is indeed an explicit reference, Deut 28:25 is almost certainly the verse referred to. Alternatively, one might view Jer 34/41:17 as the earlier text, but this verse itself seems to be a quotation from Deuteronomy. The case will be further discussed in chapter 3.

**Sol 9:9**
σὺ **ᾑρετίσω τὸ σπέρμα Αβρααμ** παρὰ πάντα τὰ ἔθνη
you chose the offspring of Abraham above all the nations

Isa 41:8
Σὺ δέ, Ισραηλ, παῖς μου Ιακωβ, ὃν ἐξελεξάμην, **σπέρμα Αβρααμ**, ὃν ἠγάπησα
but you, Israel, my servant, Iakob, whom I have chosen, the offspring of Abraam, whom I have loved
וְאַתָּה יִשְׂרָאֵל עַבְדִּי יַעֲקֹב אֲשֶׁר בְּחַרְתִּיךָ זֶרַע אַבְרָהָם אֹהֲבִי
but you, Israel, my servant, Jacob, whom I have chosen, the offspring of Abraham, my friend

34 See also Jer 25/32:17; Psalm 75/74:9.

God's promise to Abraam and his seed, i.e. his descendance, is a well-known theme (e.g. Gen 17:9, 19; 21:12; Jos 24:3), and the expression "seed of Abraham" is frequent.[35] The combination of this phrase with the notion of election is nevertheless attested in these two passages only. This makes an intertextual link likely.

The verb expressing the idea of election is not the same. The verb ἐκλέγομαι used in Isa 41:8 is the standard equivalent for Hebrew בחר "to choose, to elect" in the Septuagint. Αἱρετίζω is a less frequent equivalent.[36] Further discussion of these data will be found in chapter 4.

**Sol 10:2**
ὁ ἑτοιμάζων **νῶτον εἰς μάστιγας** καθαρισθήσεται
He who prepares his back for lashes shall be cleansed

Isa 50:6
τὸν **νῶτόν** μου δέδωκα **εἰς μάστιγας**
I have given my back to scourges

גֵּוִי נָתַתִּי לְמַכִּים

I gave my back to those who struck me

The combination of "the back" and "for lashes/scourges" is found only in these two verses in the Septuagint. Note the divergence between the MT and the Septuagint in Isa 50:6. Sol 10:2 goes with the Septuagint.

**Sol 11:1**
Σαλπίσατε ἐν Σιων ἐν **σάλπιγγι σημασίας** ἁγίων
Trumpet in Zion with a signal trumpet to summon the holy ones

Num 31:6
καὶ **αἱ σάλπιγγες τῶν σημασιῶν** ἐν ταῖς χερσὶν αὐτῶν.
And the signal trumpets were in their hands

וַחֲצֹצְרוֹת הַתְּרוּעָה בְּיָדוֹ׃

And the trumpets for sounding the alarm in his hand

2 Chr 13:12
καὶ **αἱ σάλπιγγες τῆς σημασίας** τοῦ σημαίνειν ἐφ᾽ ὑμᾶς
and the signal trumpets to signal against you

וַחֲצֹצְרוֹת הַתְּרוּעָה לְהָרִיעַ עֲלֵיכֶם

And the battle trumpets to sound the call to battle against you

35 2 Chron 20:7; Psalm 105/104:6; Sol 18:3; 3 Mac 6:3; *T.Levi* 8:15; John 8:33, 37; Rom 9:7; 11:1; 2 Cor 11:22; Gal 3:29; Heb 2:16.

36 See e.g. 1 Chron 28:4, 6, 10; 29:1, 11; Psalm 25/24:12; 119/118:130; Hag 2:23; Zec 1:17; 2:16; Ezek 20:7.

The phrase "signal trumpet" in Sol 11:1 very likely alludes to the text of Num 31:6. Nearly the same expression is found also in 2 Chr 13:12 and 1 Mac 4:40; 7:45 (both ταῖς σάλπιγξιν τῶν σημασιῶν), but those passages too would seem to be indebted to the Pentateuchal passage.

> Sol 11:2
> στῆθι, Ιερουσαλημ, ἐφ' ὑψηλοῦ καὶ **ἰδὲ τὰ τέκνα σου**
> ἀπὸ ἀνατολῶν καὶ δυσμῶν **συνηγμένα** εἰς ἅπαξ ὑπὸ κυρίου.
> Stand upon a high place, O Ierusalem, and behold your children,
> From the east and the west, gathered once again by the Lord
>
> Isa 60:4
> ἆρον κύκλῳ τοὺς ὀφθαλμούς σου καὶ **ἰδὲ συνηγμένα τὰ τέκνα σου**
> Lift up your eyes round about, and see your children gathered together
> שְׂאִי־סָבִיב עֵינַיִךְ וּרְאִי כֻּלָּם נִקְבְּצוּ
> Lift up your eyes and look around; they all gather together, they come to you

Although the word order differs, the wording of the announcement to Jerusalem that her children have been gathered back to her is identical in these two passages, thus making an allusion practically certain. Note that the textual correspondence is closer with the Septuagint version than with the Hebrew text, where the children ("sons" and "daughters") are mentioned only later in the verse.

Sol 11:2–7 finds an extensive parallel in Bar 4:36–5:8. The relation between these two passages has proved difficult to analyse and will be deferred until later in the present work (see the Appendix). The allusions to Isa 60:4 and 52:1 are present also in the parallel passage (Bar 5:5; 5:1).

> Sol 11:7
> **Ἔνδυσαι, Ιερουσαλημ, τὰ ἱμάτια τῆς δόξης σου**
> Put on, O Ierousalem, the garments of your glory
>
> Isa 52:1
> ἔνδυσαι τὴν ἰσχύν σου, Σιων, **καὶ ἔνδυσαι τὴν δόξαν σου, Ιερουσαλημ**
> Put on your strength, O Sion, and put on your glory, O Ierousalem
> לִבְשִׁי עֻזֵּךְ צִיּוֹן לִבְשִׁי בִּגְדֵי תִפְאַרְתֵּךְ יְרוּשָׁלַםִ

Put on your strength, O Zion, put on your beautiful garments,
O Jerusalem

The call to Jerusalem to dress up in Sol 11:7 shares much vocabulary with Isa 52:1 and almost certainly alludes to its text.[37] In one detail, the text of Sol 11:7 stands closer to MT than to the Septuagint: the call to put on *garments* of glory is not found in the latter. This exclusive correspondence does not necessarily indicate direct contact with the MT (see below, chapter 4).

Like the previous example, this allusion has a parallel in Bar 5:1–8 (see Bar 5:1).

**Sol 12:6**
καὶ **ἀπόλοιντο οἱ ἁμαρτωλοὶ ἀπὸ προσώπου** κυρίου ἅπαξ
and may the sinners perish altogether from the presence of thc Lord

Psalm 68/67:3
ὡς τήκεται κηρὸς ἀπὸ προσώπου πυρός, οὕτως **ἀπόλοιντο οἱ ἁμαρτωλοὶ ἀπὸ προσώπου** τοῦ θεοῦ.
as wax melts from before fire, so may sinners perish from before God.

יֹאבְדוּ רְשָׁעִים מִפְּנֵי אֱלֹהִים
as wax melts before fire, let the wicked perish before God.

While the perishing of sinners is mentioned in other passages,[38] the entire expression found in these two passages is distinctive. Note also the use of the same optative mood.

**Sol 13:5**
Ἐταράχθη ὁ εὐσεβὴς διὰ τὰ παραπτώματα αὐτοῦ, **μήποτε συμπαραληφθῇ** μετὰ τῶν ἁμαρτωλῶν
The pious man was troubled on account of his transgressions,
lest he should be taken away along with the sinners[39]

37 See Chad Reeser, "The Use of Isaiah in Psalm of Solomon 11 and Mark 1:1-15," draft paper published on Academia.edu.

38 See Psalm 37/36:20; Sol 15:12, 13; and cf. the MT of Prov 11:10.

39 All manuscripts read ἀσεβής in Sol 13:5, but Wellhausen's conjecture, εὐσεβής, has been adopted by most editors (see Albrecht, *Psalmi Salomonis*, 56). Note, however, the detailed defence of the received text in Patrick Pouchelle, "Critique textuelle et traduction du treizième Psaume de Salomon," *Journal for the Study of Judaism* 42 (2011), 508–530, in particular 515–519.

Gen 19:17

Σῴζων σῷζε τὴν σεαυτοῦ ψυχήν· μὴ περιβλέψῃς εἰς τὰ ὀπίσω μηδὲ στῇς ἐν πάσῃ τῇ περιχώρῳ· εἰς τὸ ὄρος σῴζου, **μήποτε συμπαραλημφθῇς**

In saving, save your own soul; do not look around backwards or stop in the whole region round about; get safely to the mountain that you not be included.

הִמָּלֵט עַל־נַפְשֶׁךָ אַל־תַּבִּיט אַחֲרֶיךָ וְאַל־תַּעֲמֹד בְּכָל־הַכִּכָּר הָהָרָה הִמָּלֵט פֶּן־תִּסָּפֶה

Flee for your life; do not look back or stop anywhere in the Plain; flee to the hills, or else you will be consumed.

The verb συμπαραλαμβάνω is well known in the meaning "to take along" someone on a voyage, but in these two passages its implications are altogether more ominous. What is at stake is the possibility that one should perish with sinners just because one dwells among them.[40] This was the risk the angels advised Lot to avoid, and it is the danger menacing the pious according to Sol 13:5. Thus the phrase μήποτε συμπαραληφθῇ very likely reflects conscious reference to the verse in Genesis.[41]

The words μετὰ τῶν ἁμαρτωλῶν "with the sinners" appears to confirm this conclusion. According to Gen. 13:13, the people who were in Sodom were "exceedingly sinful before God" (ἁμαρτωλοὶ ἐναντίον τοῦ θεοῦ σφόδρα).

**Sol 15:3**

καρπὸν χειλέων **ἐν ὀργάνῳ ἡρμοσμένῳ** γλώσσης

the fruit of the lips with the tuned instrument of the tongue

2 Sam/2 Kgds 6:5

καὶ Δαυιδ καὶ οἱ υἱοὶ Ισραηλ παίζοντες ἐνώπιον κυρίου **ἐν ὀργάνοις ἡρμοσμένοι**

And David and the sons of Israel were sporting before the Lord with tuned instruments

דָּוִד וְכָל־בֵּית יִשְׂרָאֵל מְשַׂחֲקִים לִפְנֵי יְהוָה בְּכֹל עֲצֵי בְרוֹשִׁים

40 On this motif, see Jan Joosten, "The Interpretation of Deuteronomy 29:17–18 in the Hellenistic Period. Septuagint, Qumran and Parabiblical Literature," in *The Dynamics of Language and Exegesis at Qumran*, ed. D. Dimant, R. G. Kratz, FAT 35 (Tübingen: Mohr Siebeck, 2009), 107–120.

41 Sol 13:5 uses the more "correct" form without *mu*, but the difference is hardly significant.

David and all the house of Israel were dancing before the LORD on all manner of instruments made of fir wood[42]

The expression ἐν ὀργάνοις ἡρμοσμένοις "with tuned instruments" is found again in 2 Sam/2 Kgds 6:14, but it is otherwise unattested in the biblical corpus. Although there is a difference in grammatical number, it seems likely that the expression in Sol 15:13 harks back to the story in 2 Sam/2 Kgds 6. Note that the Septuagint text diverges markedly from the Masoretic text.

**Sol 15:4**
**ὁ ποιῶν ταῦτα οὐ σαλευθήσεται εἰς τὸν αἰῶνα** ἀπὸ κακοῦ
he who does these things shall never be shaken by evil

Psalm 15/14:5
**ὁ ποιῶν ταῦτα οὐ σαλευθήσεται εἰς τὸν αἰῶνα.**
He who does these things shall never be shaken.
עֹשֵׂה־אֵלֶּה לֹא יִמּוֹט לְעוֹלָם

While Psalm 15 refers to ethical questions, Sol 15 refers to praise of God, but the promise attached to the recommendations is expressed in the same words.

**Sol 15:6**
ὅτι **τὸ σημεῖον** τοῦ θεοῦ ἐπὶ δικαίους εἰς σωτηρίαν
for the mark of God is upon the righteous for salvation

**Sol 15:9**
**τὸ** γὰρ **σημεῖον** τῆς ἀπωλείας **ἐπὶ** τοῦ **μετώπου** αὐτῶν
for the mark of destruction is upon their forehead.

Ezek 9:4
δὸς **τὸ σημεῖον ἐπὶ τὰ μέτωπα** τῶν ἀνδρῶν τῶν καταστεναζόντων καὶ τῶν κατωδυνωμένων ἐπὶ πάσαις ταῖς ἀνομίαις ταῖς γινομέναις ἐν μέσῳ αὐτῆς
give the mark upon the foreheads of the men who sigh and have been afflicted over all the lawless acts that happen in their midst
וְהִתְוִיתָ תָּו עַל־מִצְחוֹת הָאֲנָשִׁים הַנֶּאֱנָחִים וְהַנֶּאֱנָקִים עַל כָּל־הַתּוֹעֵבוֹת הַנַּעֲשׂוֹת בְּתוֹכָהּ
put a mark on the foreheads of those who sigh and groan over all the abominations that are committed in it

42 NRSV "...with all their might, with songs," following 1 Chron 13:8 and 4QSam[a].

In Ezekiel only the righteous get a mark on their forehead. Nevertheless, the motif and the vocabulary used to express it are striking enough to make a literary allusion nearly certain.

**Sol 16:1**
Ἐν τῷ **νυστάξαι ψυχήν μου** ἀπὸ κυρίου παρὰ μικρὸν ὠλίσθησα
When my soul slumbered, away from the Lord, I slipped for a short time

Psalm 119/118:28
**ἔνυσταξεν ἡ ψυχή μου** ἀπὸ ἀκηδίας[43]
My soul was drowsy from exhaustion

דָּלְפָה נַפְשִׁי מִתּוּגָה

My soul melts away for sorrow

The combination of the verb νυστάζω "to become sleepy" and ψυχή "soul" is found only in these two passages in the Septuagint.

**Sol 16:2**
παρ᾽ ὀλίγον **ἐξεχύθη ἡ ψυχή** μου **εἰς θάνατον**
But for a little my soul was poured out to death

Isa 53:12
ἀνθ᾽ ὧν **παρεδόθη εἰς θάνατον ἡ ψυχὴ** αὐτοῦ
because his soul was given over to death

תַּחַת אֲשֶׁר הֶעֱרָה לַמָּוֶת נַפְשׁוֹ

because he poured out himself (lit. "his soul") to death

Ryle and James state: "The passage Isai. liii. 12, 'he poured out his soul unto death,' may have originated the phrase in our verse."[44] The thought and part of the vocabulary of Sol 16:2 closely conform to the well-known verse from Isaiah.

However, the verb used in the Psalm differs from that of the Septuagint of Isa 53:12. Ryle and James add: "But in that case the translator has followed the Hebrew and not the LXX." Indeed, "to pour out" is one of the meanings of ערה *hiphil* (see further in chapter 4).

**Sol 16:9**
**Τὰ ἔργα τῶν χειρῶν** μου **κατεύθυνον** ἐν τόπῳ σου
Direct the works of my hands in your place

43 With an eye on the Hebrew, Rahlfs edited the verb as ἔσταξεν "dripped," a reading attested for the Quinta and the Sexta. All Septuagint manuscripts have ἔνυσταξεν.

44 *Psalms of the Pharisees*, 118.

Psalm 90/89:17

**τὰ ἔργα τῶν χειρῶν** ἡμῶν **κατεύθυνον** ἐφ᾽ ἡμᾶς

prosper upon us the work of our hand

וּמַעֲשֵׂה יָדֵינוּ כּוֹנְנָה עָלֵינוּ

prosper for us the work of our hands

The combination of the verb κατευθύνω "to prosper, cause to prosper, go straight" with the expression "the work of the hands" is found only in these two passages, making a direct reference very likely.

**Sol 17:1**

ἐν σοί, ὁ θεός, καυχήσεται **ἡ ψυχὴ** ἡμῶν

In you, O God, shall our soul boast

Psalm 34/33:3

**ἐν** τῷ κυρίῳ **ἐπαινεσθήσεται ἡ ψυχή** μου

In the Lord my soul shall commend itself[45]

בַּיהוָה תִּתְהַלֵּל נַפְשִׁי

My soul makes its boast in the LORD

When one looks only at the Septuagint version of Psalm 34/33:3, the verses do not seem to be particularly close. However, once we realize that Hebrew התהלל is regularly rendered with καυχάομαι, the similarity leaps to the eye.[46] The notion of the soul of the singer "boasting" in God is found only in these two passages.

Note that Aquila corrected **ἐπαινεσθήσεται** to καυχήσεται "shall boast," bringing the verse in Psalms closer to the one in Sol 17 (see further chapter 4).

**Sol 17:3**

ἡμεῖς **δὲ** ἐλπιοῦμεν **ἐπὶ τὸν θεὸν σωτῆρα ἡμῶν**

But we will hope in God our savior

Mic 7:7

Εγὼ **δὲ** ἐπὶ τὸν κύριον ἐπιβλέψομαι, ὑπομενῶ **ἐπὶ τῷ θεῷ τῷ σωτῆρί** μου

But as for me, I will look to the Lord; I will wait for God my savior

וַאֲנִי בַּיהוָה אֲצַפֶּה אוֹחִילָה לֵאלֹהֵי יִשְׁעִי

But as for me, I will look to the LORD, I will wait for the God of my salvation

---

45 NETS: "in the Lord my soul shall be recommended."

46 See 1 Kgs 21/3 Kgds 20:11; Psalm 49/48:7; Prov 25:14; Jer 9:22.

The thought expressed in these two verses is similar, but the vocabulary is only partly so. However, the meanings of ἐλπίζω and ὑπομένω overlap, and the Hebrew verb translated in Mic 7:7 by means of the latter is in other passages rendered with the former.[47] On the whole, it seems likely that Sol 17:3 is formulated in reference to the passage in Micah.

**Sol 17:7**
Καὶ σύ, ὁ θεός, καταβαλεῖς αὐτοὺς καὶ ἀρεῖς τὸ σπέρμα αὐτῶν ἀπὸ τῆς γῆς
ἐν τῷ ἐπαναστῆναι αὐτοῖς **ἄνθρωπον ἀλλότριον** γένους ἡμῶν
But you, O God, will overthrow them and will remove their offspring from the earth,
when there rises up against them a person that is foreign to our race

Deut 17:15
οὐ δυνήσῃ καταστῆσαι ἐπὶ σεαυτὸν **ἄνθρωπον ἀλλότριον**, ὅτι οὐκ ἀδελφός σού ἐστιν
You shall not have power to appoint a strange person, because he is not your brother.
לֹא תוּכַל לָתֵת עָלֶיךָ אִישׁ נָכְרִי אֲשֶׁר לֹא־אָחִיךָ הוּא
you are not permitted to put a foreigner over you, who is not your brother

Both ἄνθρωπος and ἀλλότριος are common words in the Septuagint, but their combination in a single noun phrase is limited to these two passages. Note also that there is thematic similarity between the two passages: the Israelites should not make a foreigner king over them (Deut 17:15), but now a foreigner has risen up to rule over them (Sol 17:7). All in all, the intertextual connection between the two passages seems likely.

**Sol 17:15**
Καὶ ἐπεκρατοῦσαν αὐτῶν **οἱ υἱοὶ τῆς διαθήκης** ἐν μέσῳ ἐθνῶν **συμμίκτων**
And the sons of the covenant surpassed them in the midst of motley nations

Ezek 30:5
Πέρσαι καὶ Κρῆτες καὶ Λυδοὶ καὶ Λίβυες καὶ πάντες οἱ **ἐπίμικτοι** καὶ **τῶν υἱῶν τῆς διαθήκης** μου μαχαίρᾳ πεσοῦνται ἐν αὐτῇ

47 See notably Psalm 38/37:15; 42/41:5; 130/129:5-6 (all *hiphil*).

Persians and Cretans and Lydians and Lybians and all those mixed in and some of the sons of my covenant shall fall in it by dagger

כּוּשׁ וּפוּט וְלוּד וְכָל־הָעֶרֶב וְכוּב וּבְנֵי אֶרֶץ הַבְּרִית אִתָּם בַּחֶרֶב יִפֹּלוּ

Ethiopia, and Put, and Lud, and all Arabia, and Libya, and the people of the allied land shall fall with them by the sword.

The expression "son/sons of the/my covenant" is not attested in the Hebrew Bible and these are the only two occurrences of the phrase in the Septuagint.[48] The fact that both passages also mention a "mixed" ethnic group makes a literary connection between them nearly certain. Admittedly, apart from the phraseology, the two passages do not seem to have anything in common.

**Sol 17:21**

Ιδέ, κύριε, καὶ **ἀνάστησον αὐτοῖς τὸν βασιλέα αὐτῶν** υἱὸν **Δαυιδ**

See, O Lord, and raise up for them their king, the son of Dauid

Jer 30/37:9

καὶ ἐργῶνται τῷ κυρίῳ θεῷ αὐτῶν, καὶ τὸν **Δαυιδ βασιλέα αὐτῶν ἀναστήσω αὐτοῖς**

And they shall work for the Lord, their God, and I will raise up Dauid as their king for them.

וְעָבְדוּ אֵת יְהוָה אֱלֹהֵיהֶם וְאֵת דָּוִד מַלְכָּם אֲשֶׁר אָקִים לָהֶם

And they shall serve the Lord their God and David their king, whom I will raise up for them.

In spite of the difference between "David" and "son of David," there can be no doubt that Sol 17 here harks back to the passage in Jeremiah.

**Sol 17:23–24**

ἐκτρῖψαι ὑπερηφανίαν ἁμαρτωλοῦ **ὡς σκεύη κεραμέως,**
**ἐν ῥάβδῳ σιδηρᾷ συντρῖψαι** πᾶσαν ὑπόστασιν αὐτῶν
to smash the arrogance of the sinner like a potter's vessel,
to shatter all their substance with an iron rod.

Psalm 2:9

ποιμανεῖς αὐτοὺς **ἐν ῥάβδῳ σιδηρᾷ,**
**ὡς σκεῦος κεραμέως συντρίψεις** αὐτούς.
You shall shepherd them with an iron rod,
and like a potter's vessel you will shatter them.

48 The expression is found a few times in the Dead Sea Scrolls (e.g. 1QM 17:8) and in Acts 3:25. It is frequent also in Syriac sources.

תְּרֹעֵם בְּשֵׁבֶט בַּרְזֶל כִּכְלִי יוֹצֵר תְּנַפְּצֵם
You shall break them with a rod of iron
you shall dash them in pieces like a potter's vessel

The common imagery and vocabulary of the two passages more than suffices to demonstrate an intertextual link between them.

Note, however, that Sol 17:23–24 does not pick up on the shepherding theme expressed in the Septuagint, and thus aligns with the MT specifically. This configuration will be discussed in more detail in chapter 4.

Sol 17:27
**οὐκ** ἀφήσει **ἀδικίαν** ἐν μέσῳ αὐτῶν **αὐλισθῆναι** ἔτι
he shall not allow injustice to lodge in their midst any longer,

Job 11:14
**ἀδικία** δὲ ἐν διαίτῃ σου **μὴ αὐλισθήτω**
let no injustice lodge in your dwelling
וְאַל־תַּשְׁכֵּן בְּאֹהָלֶיךָ עַוְלָה
do not let wickedness reside in your tents.

The collocation of αὐλίζομαι "to lodge, spend the night" with ἀδικία "injustice" is found only in these two passages, thus indicating a literary connection.

Although αὐλίζομαι "to lodge, spend the night" is used occasionally in late Greek to situate inanimate objects (blood, winds), the metaphorical use exemplified in these passages is not found in non-biblical Greek. In the Septuagint, the usage occurs elsewhere, with "weeping," Psalm 30/29:6, or "error," Job 19:4.[49]

Sol 17:30
Καὶ ἕξει **λαοὺς** ἐθνῶν **δουλεύειν αὐτῷ ὑπὸ** τὸν **ζυγὸν** αὐτοῦ
And he shall have the peoples of the nations to be subject to him under his yoke

Zeph 3:9
ὅτι τότε μεταστρέψω ἐπὶ **λαοὺς** γλῶσσαν εἰς γενεὰν αὐτῆς τοῦ ἐπικαλεῖσθαι πάντας τὸ ὄνομα κυρίου τοῦ **δουλεύειν αὐτῷ ὑπὸ ζυγὸν** ἕνα.

49 See also Sol 3:6, which has elements from Job 11:14 and Isa 30:1 (see the discussion of Sol 3:10 above).

Because then I will change the tongue for peoples in its generation, that all might call upon the name of the Lord to be subject to him under one yoke

כִּי־אָז אֶהְפֹּךְ אֶל־עַמִּים שָׂפָה בְרוּרָה לִקְרֹא כֻלָּם בְּשֵׁם יְהוָה לְעָבְדוֹ שְׁכֶם אֶחָד

At that time I will change the speech of the peoples to a pure speech, that all of them may call on the name of the LORD and serve him with one accord.

In spite of a few differences, the statement in Sol 17:30 is almost certainly dependent on the prophecy of Zephaniah. Note that the allusion agrees specifically with the Septuagint, while the MT of Zeph 3:9 speaks of "one shoulder" instead of "one yoke."

**Sol 17:33b**

**οὐδὲ πληθυνεῖ αὐτῷ χρυσίον** οὐδὲ **ἀργύριον** εἰς πόλεμον

Nor shall he multiply for himself gold and silver

Deut 17:17

καὶ **ἀργύριον** καὶ **χρυσίον οὐ πληθυνεῖ ἑαυτῷ** σφόδρα

also silver and gold he shall not multiply exceedingly for himself

וְכֶסֶף וְזָהָב לֹא יַרְבֶּה־לּוֹ מְאֹד

silver and gold he must not acquire in great quantity for himself

The collocation of five identical (or nearly identical) words makes the allusion a certainty. Moreover, both texts speak about the king of Israel.

Sol 17:33a makes reference to the fact that the Messiah will not put his hope in horse and rider and bow, alluding to Deut 17:16 more loosely.

**Sol 17:35**

**πατάξει** γὰρ **γῆν τῷ λόγῳ τοῦ στόματος αὐτοῦ** εἰς αἰῶνα

For he shall strike the earth with the word of his mouth forever

Isa 11:4

καὶ **πατάξει γῆν τῷ λόγῳ τοῦ στόματος αὐτοῦ**

And he shall strike the earth with the word of his mouth

וְהִכָּה־אֶרֶץ בְּשֵׁבֶט פִּיו

And he shall strike the earth with the rod of his mouth.

Of all the references to scripture, this one and the one in Sol 15:4 are the only ones that arguably constitute a quotation.

Note that the Septuagint version of Isa 11:4 has decoded part of the metaphor: the *rod* of the mouth has become the *word* of the mouth. Sol 17:35 follows the Septuagint.

## 1.2. Analysis

Our list counts 50 cases. It is advisable to take this figure with a pinch of salt. Some of the examples listed may be rejected, or, perhaps more probably, a few instances omitted due to oversight or excessive caution may have to be added.[50] It is nevertheless worthwhile considering the number against the total number of verses of the corpus which is just shy of 300.[51]

The instances are fairly evenly distributed, although Sol 17 definitely stands out with its 10 cases. In detail, the distribution of scriptural allusions in the Psalms of Solomon is as follows:

| | |
|---|---|
| 1:3 | 10:2 |
| 2:8, 12, 17, 18, 20 | 11:1, 2, 7 |
| 3:2, 4, 8, 10, 12 | 12:6 |
| 4:3, 19, 20 | 13:5 |
| 5:2, 3, 5, 12, 19 | 15:1, 3, 5, 6+9 |
| 7:3, 6 | 16:1, 2, 9 |
| 8:2, 9, 14a, 14b | 17:1, 3, 7, 15, 21, 23–24, 27, 30, 33, 35 |
| 9:2, 9 | |

As was noted above, the examples included in the list have been selected because they are fairly certain. This is necessary if we want to build upon them in order to develop historical and text-historical observations. Many expressions have not been included although they do to some degree or other remind one of scriptural passages.[52] Indeed, the attentive reader of the entire corpus soon realizes that scriptural diction is present throughout, even if it is not always possible to pinpoint its origin. This remark may be illustrated with a few examples.

50 Some borderline cases have been excluded: Sol 2:26, perhaps alluding to the language of Isa 14:19; Sol 4:7 and Psalm 44/43:14; Sol 17:10 and Psalm 145/144:13b (*nun* strophe in alphabetic acrostic, which has dropped out of the MT by accident). Note also the possible presence of an allusion to Isa 40:4; 45:2 in Sol 11 (see Appendix).

51 In Albrecht's edition I counted 293 verses.

52 E.g. Sol 10:5 Δίκαιος καὶ ὅσιος ὁ κύριος is close to Deut 32:4, but also to Psalm 145/144:17.

According to the list, there are no cases in Sol 6; 14 and 18. This should not be interpreted to mean that these Psalms are bereft of scriptural language. Note the following random sampling from Sol 6:

**Sol 6:1**
ἡ καρδία αὐτοῦ ἑτοίμη "his heart is prepared"
Cf. ἑτοίμη ἡ καρδία "the heart is ready" in Psalms 57/56:8; 108/107:2; 112/111:7

It is impossible to indicate the Psalm that provided the authors of Sol 6 with the motif of the "prepared heart." Consequently it hard to be certain that this is an allusion at all. It may be a phrase the authors were familiar with, perhaps from the liturgical language of their community. Although it probably does go back to Psalms, it may do so indirectly.

**Sol 6:2**
αἱ ὁδοὶ αὐτοῦ κατευθύνονται ὑπὸ κυρίου "his ways are directed by the Lord"

Cf. Psalm 37/36:23
παρὰ κυρίου τὰ διαβήματα ἀνθρώπου κατευθύνεται "a person's steps are directed by the Lord"

The thought in these two verses is rather close and some of the vocabulary overlaps. However, the combination of κατευθύνομαι with διάβημα or ὁδός is found several times in the Septuagint.[53]

**Sol 6:6**
ὁ ποιῶν ἔλεος τοῖς ἀγαπῶσίν αὐτόν "who works pity for those who love him"

Cf. Exod 20:6; Deut 5:10
καὶ ποιῶν ἔλεος εἰς χιλιάδας τοῖς ἀγαπῶσίν με "doing mercy to thousands for those who love me"

The two clauses are similar, but the most salient phrase of Exod 20:6; Deut 5:10, "to thousands," is missing in Sol 6:6. Note that "to do mercy" is a recurrent expression in the Septuagint, "those who love the Lord" is similarly frequent, and the association of "pity" with "those who love the Lord" is found in several other passages but the Ten Commandments.[54]

53 See Psalm 40/39:3; Ps 119/118:133.

54 See Deut 7:9; Neh 1:5; Dan 9:4; and compare Sol 4:25; 10:3. An additional case of this type is the possible allusion to Deut 28:49 in Sol 8:15 "He brought him from the end of the earth": the two passages have several

These cases show up the difficulty in deciding between an instance of biblical diction and an allusion to a specific passage.

The distribution over the biblical books is unsurprising: Psalms predominates, the Pentateuch and the Latter Prophets are well represented, and there is a sprinkling of cases from the historical books and other writings.

Gen 19:17
Exod 17:14
Lev 5:18
Num 25:4 ; 31:6
Deut 17:7, 15, 17; 28:25
1 Sam/1 Kgds 2:5
2 Sam/2 Kgds 6:5
1 Kgs 20:3 / 3 Kgds 21:3
Isa 11:4; 19:14; 21:1; 30:1; 41:8; 49:24; 50:6; 52:1; 53:12; 59:2; 60:4
Jer 23/32:15; 30/37:9
Ezek 3:12; 9:4; 22:7; 30:5; 43:7
Hos 10:10
Micah 7:7
Zeph 3:9
Psalms 2:9; 7:12; 15/14:5; 28/27:1; 18/17:7; 34/33:3; 53/52:6; 68/67:3; 86/85:5; 90/89:17; 119/118:28; 147/146:1
Prov 3:11; 30:17
Job 11:14
Dan 12:2

Books missing from this list should not for that reason be considered unknown to, or unrecognized by, the authors. For instance, although there are no certain references to any Minor Prophets other than Hosea, Micah and Zephaniah the authors surely knew the entire book of the Twelve. They may similarly have known books such as Joshua, Judges or Ezra-Nehemiah without finding an occasion to allude to their text.

---

expressions in common, but these same expressions are found also elsewhere in the Septuagint (note e.g. Jer 6:22).

# 2.
# Uses of Scripture in the Psalms of Solomon

The allusions in Psalms of Solomon listed in the preceding chapter show beyond the shadow of a doubt that ancient religious texts were important to the authors and their community. This being so, one can only be struck by the freedom with which scripture is treated. While the authors make a show of referring to texts they consider authoritative, they hardly ever quote them verbatim.

This freedom in adapting the texts tends to hamper text-historical analysis. When looking for meaningful readings, scholars must first sift out variation that was introduced by the author of the Psalms of Solomon. As will be seen in the following chapters, enough features remain that enable analysis of the type that will be attempted in this book. Nevertheless, it will pay to know as much as possible about the way the authors handle the scriptural text. In this perspective, we will in the present chapter explore the intertextual dynamics of the corpus in some detail. The material foundation of the discussion will be the allusions identified in chapter 1, but other features of intertextuality will be considered along the way.

The "biblicizing" style of the Psalms of Solomon may strike some as lacking in originality. If the authors have something new to say, why do they clothe their thoughts in scriptural language? In seeking an answer to this question it is important to realize that the authors' relation to scripture is not imitative as much as it is anthological. In order to express their thoughts and feelings, hopes and aspirations, the authors select words and expressions from earlier texts. Their piety leads them to take the older writings as a springboard from which to develop their own thought; their learnedness authorizes them to give new meaning to fragments of scripture. To the authors of the Psalms of Solomon, scripture is less like a code imposed upon them from the outside than like a discourse that they recognize as their own; less like a precious heirloom to be passed on to later generations than like a home they were born into and still inhabit.

## 2.1. Psalms of Solomon as an extension of scripture

An immediate effect of the dense presence of scriptural language in the Psalms of Solomon is to make the corpus look like scripture. Psalms of Solomon is not a pseudepigraphic writing in the sense that it seriously pretends to be written by a scriptural character.[1] Nor does it even pretend to pretend, as in Wisdom of Solomon, written *de ore Solomonis* as an acknowledged literary device.[2] Nothing of the sort can be found in the Psalms of Solomon.[3] The corpus does not seek to appear older than it is. It rather openly refers to current events such as Pompey's occupation of Jerusalem and his death in Egypt. The authors speak in their own voice about moral and religious issues that are of concern to them. If they fail to name Pompey or the Romans, this is not because they want to hide their message, but because of the style form they have selected.

Nonetheless, the entire discourse is stylized as an extension of scripture. The world we enter as we read is the biblical one. Everything started with the creation of heaven and earth (8:7). The creator God soon elected the family of Abraham out of all the nations and made a covenant with the patriarchs (9:9–10).[4] The chosen people, Israel,

1 See the statement of Marinus de Jonge, *Outside the Old Testament* (Cambridge: CUP, 1985), p. 159: "Nothing in these songs warrants an ascription to the famous son of David. They are not even pseudepigraphical in the usual sense of the word. The psalms proper do not hint at any connection with Solomon and the circumstances in which he reigned." A different view has been argued by Gordley, though hardly in a compelling way, see Matthew E. Gordley, "Psalms of Solomon as Solomonic Discourse: The Nature and Function of Attribution to Solomon in a Pseudonymous Psalm Collection," *JSP* 25 (2015), 52–88. See further below in section 2.5.

2 On Wisdom of Solomon, see the brilliant study of Judith Newman, "The Democratization of Kingship in Wisdom of Solomon," in *The Idea of Biblical Interpretation: Essays in Honor of James L. Kugel*, ed. Hindy Najman and Judith Newman, SJSJ 83 (Leiden: Brill, 2003), 309–328.

3 On a possible rationale for the attribution of the corpus to Solomon see below in section 2.5.

4 Note also Jacob in Sol 7:10; 15:1.

were given a land that had belonged to other nations before them (9:1; 1:8).[5] Their life was to be regulated perpetually by commandments that God had given to them (14:2, 5). Jerusalem, the consistent focus of the authors' attention, is the city of God's sanctuary (8:4).[6] God also elected David to be Israel's king (17:4). In later times, Israel was taken into exile, and dispersed among the nations (9:1-2). But God is already gathering the diaspora (11:2; 8:28), and in the near future God will reestablish Israel as a kingdom, ruled by a descendant of David and dominating the entire earth (17:26-44).

What these multiple references accomplish is not to transport the readers to the time of the ancestors, but on the contrary, to suggest that the scriptural parameters are still valid for them. Scripture has a grip on the present. The Roman occupants are referred to as "nations," because that is what they are in scriptural language. Pompey is called "the dragon" because he is viewed through the lens of the prophecies of Ezekiel.[7]

The language of the corpus strongly coheres with this scriptural mode of presentation. Much of the vocabulary bears the stamp of ancestral writings. Words such as "creation," "law," "covenant," "atonement" and "blessing," are used with a distinctive meaning, richly defined in scripture. These words are not multipurpose items of vocabulary, but tokens of a scriptural terminology that could be fully appreciated only by those familiar with the writings of Israel. Likewise, expressions such as "to hide the face," "to fear God," "to harden the neck" or "the arm of the Lord" immediately evoke scripture. And again, these expressions do not generally point back to the past. The scriptural language is used to describe and assess the present.

A similar point can be made about the poetic style. Many stylistic features are reminiscent of scripture, notably Psalms. The organizing principle is the coupling of lines, with an occasional triplet. A somewhat freewheeling use of poetic parallelism can be observed throughout the corpus:

> **Sol 1:4**
> Their wealth was spread over the whole earth,

5 The name Israel occurs 30 times in the corpus.
6 The name Jerusalem is mentioned 20 times, Sion only once in 11:1.
7 See notably Ezek 32:2, 5.

and their glory to the end of the earth

**Sol 5:11**
You feed kings and rulers and peoples, O God,
and who is the hope of the poor and needy, unless it be you,
O Lord?

Several other stylistic features recall biblical poetry, such as sudden changes of grammatical person (e.g. 4:1-3), apostrophe (e.g. 2:32), personification and imagined speech (e.g. 1:1-7). All of these features lend the Psalms of Solomon a biblical ring.

Express allusions play a crucial part in the scripturalization of discourse. Several allusions appear to serve no other purpose than to enrich the language with scriptural overtones. Seeking a suitable curse on the hypocrites, who are the butt of criticism in all of Sol 4, the authors come up with "may ravens peck out [their] eyes" (4:20), quoted almost verbatim from Prov 30:17. The role of the allusion in this case does not go beyond satisfying the reader that the latter-day hypocrites are cursed with a biblical imprecation. There is no reason to think that the hypocrites are compared to those who dishonor their parents, the topic of Prov 30:17. In Sol 8, God punishes the leading classes of Jerusalem for their hidden sins by "mixing for them a spirit of confusion" (8:14a), which leads them against all reason to open the gates of the city to the enemy. The divine punishment is formulated in words taken wholesale from Isa 19:14, but again, as it seems, without other implications. All the allusion is intended to accomplish is to remind one of scripture. Similar use of phrases lifted from scripture to give the discourse a scriptural veneer without doing much else are found throughout the corpus.[8]

## 2.2. Fitting the present into a scriptural mold

While addressing the real situation of their community, the authors use scriptural language so as to suggest continuity between the times of old and the present. In this perspective, some scriptural allusions are made to do more work. An allusion may implicitly assimilate an issue from the time of the authors to a scriptural antecedent, thus

8 Additional examples are the scriptural allusions in Sol 2:20; 8:2 and 15:3 (see chapter 1).

suggesting that the two worlds, the biblical one and the present one, are commensurate. At times, this procedure puts some strain on both the present reality and the biblical text referred to. Alongside an ostensible analogy there are also some elements that seem poorly matched. A few examples will illustrate the dynamics involved.

> **Sol 13:5**
> The pious man was troubled on account of his transgressions,
> lest he should be taken away along with the sinners.

The problem of sin looms large in our corpus. One recurrent motif is the need for the pious to contain it: to implore divine help in staying away from it, to avoid repeating sinful behavior, and to seek release from sins committed. Sol 13:5 is a perfect expression of this theme: the pious one worries about his missteps, because they make him resemble the sinners who will be taken away.

The allusion to Gen 19:17 adds another dimension to the discourse. Gen 19 too speaks about a person, Lot, at risk of being taken away along with sinners—the inhabitants of Sodom. The allusion draws attention to this analogy. Perhaps it encompasses the notion that the sinners in Jerusalem are incorrigible, like the inhabitants of Sodom, and that a similar fate awaits them. Beyond these similarities, however, the two texts differ in important respects. Lot's problem was that God had decided to wipe out the city where he resided entirely. If he and his family remained there, they would be killed together with the sinful whatever the degree of their own sinfulness. It was a matter of collective punishment, or at the most, guilt by association. This is different from the situation envisaged in Sol 13. The fear of the pious is not that they will be in the wrong place at the wrong time, nor that they will be declared guilty by association. What they fear is the effect of sin, which assimilates them to the wicked. If they, although pious, behave like the sinners, the same end may await them. In light of this difference, the analogy between Lot and the pious turns out to be rather strained.

The dissimilarity did not bother the authors. To them what counted was to present their concerns in scriptural terms, and thus to draw their own existence into the world of the biblical heroes.

> **Sol 2:12**
> Before the sun they paraded their injustices

Sol 2:11-13 is a difficult passage of which widely divergent translations have been proposed. Most commentators nevertheless agree that it describes how the Romans treated those Jerusalemites who had resisted Pompey's occupation of the city.[9] The subject of the verb παρεδειγμάτισαν is not spelled out. Some take the clause to mean that the Jews paraded their own injustices, but this does not seem to fit the context. The preceding verse certainly refers to what the enemy did to their captives ("they set [them] to be mocked").[10] Note also that verse 17 affirms that God has exposed (ἀνεκάλυψας) the sins of the Jerusalemites, which must therefore have been done in secret, not paraded before the sun. Paul de Lagarde proposed to make God the subject and read παρεδειγμάτισεν.[11] This conjecture has not been widely adopted, but it contains a moment of truth: the "injustices" that are paraded are not resistance against the Romans, but offenses against God. The most likely reading is that the unnamed Romans are the subject of the verb, and that they are viewed as instruments of God's justice. "The Gentiles are carrying out the Divine judgement in making an open show of Jewish iniquities."[12]

This reading is buttressed by the reference to Num 25:4. In Numbers, the people "profane themselves" (ἐβεβηλώθη) with the daughters of Moab and they participate in cultic acts in honor of Baal Peor. God then commands Moses to take the leaders of the people and "make an example of them to the LORD before the sun." The association with Num 25 suggests:

- The sins of the Jerusalemites are of the same type as those of the Israelites at Baal Peor: sexual and cultic impropriety.
- Punishment for sins of this type, although carried out by human hands, is ordained expressly by God.

9 For the historical background of the events, see Sharon, *Judea under Roman Domination*, 88–99; 401–423.

10 The text is uncertain, a few manuscripts read the verb in the singular. Contextually, however, the grammatical subject must be the enemy, not God.

11 Lagarde's proposal is quoted as a personal communication in Adolf Hilgenfeld, *Messias Iudaeorum: libris eorum Paulo ante et Paulo post Christum natum conscriptis illustratus* (Leipzig: Sumptu Fuesiano, 1869), 4.

12 Ryle & James, *Psalms of the Pharisees*, 16.

- The punishment is directed toward the leading classes who are ultimately responsible for the crisis,
- its main implication is public shame.

Thus the allusion to Num 25:4 contributes toward the authors' goal of relating recent events to scriptural models. The society they inhabit may look very different from that of the Pentateuch, but on a deeper level the two worlds are congruent. In fact, they are the same: to the authors of Sol, what happens to them and their contemporaries is but an extension of biblical paradigms.

To modern readers, the claim implicit in the allusion to Num 25:4 may seem overblown, even arbitrary. In historical terms, the Roman occupation of Jerusalem in 63 BCE had almost nothing in common with the events narrated in Num 25. The claim is perfectly in tune, however, with the style and discursive mode of the corpus as a whole.

> **Sol 5:3**
> For no one will take booty from a strong man.

Sol 5 is a coherent unit entirely devoted to the notion of divine providence: God will give to all creatures their part, which the pious should receive with joy and thanksgiving.[13] Part of the argument is that there is no reason to worry, as God will provide in sufficiency, nor to wish for more, as abundance will lead to sin.

The allusion to Isa 49:24 ties in with this last motif. Humans will not be able to increase their share beyond what God has decided to give, "for no one can take booty from a strong man." God is generous, but also incomparably powerful. The analogy between Sol 5:3 and the text alluded to is even more strained than in the preceding example. In Isaiah 49, the topic is God's capacity to liberate the captive Judeans from Babylonia. This seems difficult to human eyes, but it is feasible because "no one can take booty from a strong man." The captives are God's property, and the Babylonians cannot take them away.[14] Many nuances of the text alluded to have no relevance to Sol 5 at all: the

13 See Patrick Pouchelle, "The Simple Bare Necessities: Is *Pss. Sol.* 5 a Wisdom Prayer?" in *Tracing Sapiential Traditions in Ancient Judaism*, ed. Hindy Najman, J.-S. Rey, E.J.C. Tigchelaar, JSJSupp 174 (Leiden: Brill, 2016), 138–154.

14 This is how the author of Sol 5 seems to have understood the passage; the meaning in its own context may be different. See John Goldingay, David

notion of "booty" is at home in a debate on bringing home captives, but hardly in a philosophical consideration of divine providence. The figure of the "strong man," too, fits the martial picture evoked in Isaiah, but it seems strangely inapposite in Sol 5. Even the notion of "taking" is hardly the right one in the latter context. The one and only possible point of comparison, is that of divine control.

The inappositeness did not bother the authors of Sol 5. They may not have perceived it at all. To them God's providence was displayed in the gift of their daily bread as it had been in the liberation of the exiles from Babylon. No more of a struggle was involved in the latter, and no less of a show of power in the former. Their own day-to-day existence was of one piece with the homecoming announced by the prophet.

Several other examples could be presented that work in similar ways. But these few examples may suffice to clarify the principal tendencies. The authors are like lovers of antiques who use old pots and pans as plant-holders. Contours of Scripture are forced onto the experience of the pious who recite the Psalms of Solomon. Potential mismatches are less important to the authors and their community than the sheer presence of the scriptural motif.

## 2.3. Developing scriptural ideas

In other passages the use of scripture is much more organic. Genuine motifs of scripture are expanded to make them fruitful to the later epoch. Much of the corpus is oriented towards this goal: to show the enduring validity and relevance of biblical themes.

Using scripture in developing one's own arguments may seem rather similar to fitting one's world into a scriptural mold. Certainly the procedures partly overlap, and some instances could possibly be classified under either head. Nevertheless, the two phenomena need to be distinguished on the theoretical level. If the procedure described in 2.2. is like home-owners who use old cooking pots as flower stands to give their interior an ancient look, the examples in the present section are more like a gourmet chef returning to ancient foods because they

Payne, *Isaiah 40-55*, Volume II, ICC (London & New York: T&T Clark, 2006), 195–197.

are healthier and more adapted to the climate. The former procedure focuses on literary form, the latter on theological substance.

Some instances in which our corpus develops central ideas from hints in scripture are well known. The main contribution of the Psalms of Solomon to the history of ideas is the eschatological messianism it develops in Sol 17. This is a theological creation of the first order. Yet, far from presenting their doctrine of the Messiah as an original inspiration, the authors of Sol 17 derive it from scripture. The election of David and his dynasty (17:4) harks back to the prophecy of Nathan as recounted in 2 Sam 7. The call on God to raise up a descendant of David to reign over Israel again (17:21) also has antecedents in scripture.[15] The most innovative part of the Psalm, the eschatological description of the acts of the Messiah (17:22-45), is entirely derived from scriptural models, with explicit allusions playing a crucial part:

- Psalm 2:9, alluded to in 17:23-24, serves to legitimize the program of eradicating the wicked—foreign and native alike—from the territory of Israel.
- Deut 17:17, alluded to in 17:33, comes to undergird the idea that the Messiah's universal power should remain subordinate to God. In a sense, the Messiah will be like the pious authors themselves in seeking moderation and trusting in the Lord (see further below in section 2.5).
- Isa 11:4, alluded to in 17:35, motivates another important idea: the primacy of the word. The Messiah will execute his reign by blessing God and reprimanding the wicked.[16]

Many other intertexts can be suspected in Sol 17, but it is unnecessary to enumerate them all.[17] These three marked allusions suffice to show how the authors take hold of scriptural motifs and elaborate their own views from there.

---

15 See the extensive discussion in John Collins, *The Scepter and the Star. Messianism in Light of the Dead Sea Scrolls* (Grand Rapids MI: Eerdmans, $2010^2$), 52–60.

16 See Sol 17:25, 26, 29, 30, 35, 36, 38, 43. See further in section 2.5.

17 See Collins (note 15); Joseph Trafton, "What Would David Do? Messianic Expectation and Surprise in Ps. Sol. 17," in *The Psalms of Solomon: Language, History, Theology, Proceedings of the First International Meeting on the Psalms of Solomon, Strasbourg June 17–18, 2013*, ed. E. Bons, P. Pouchelle, EJL 40 (Atlanta: SBL, 2015), 155–174.

A theme that looms large throughout the Psalms of Solomon is that of divine education. Many passages are concerned with the way God educates the chosen people, and in particular the self-styled devout that produced the corpus. The conception is rooted in scripture, where God is presented as a father bringing up his son, Israel, and where all kinds of events in history and human life are interpreted as divine punishment for misdeeds and faulty attitudes.[18] The Psalms of Solomon innovate in making the pedagogical aspect central to their theology.[19] They also develop a specific vocabulary to express it. The words παιδεύω, παιδεία, παιδευτής are prominent, and other words such as ἐλέγχω/ἐλεγμός "to reprove," κατευθύνω "to direct," νουθετέω "to admonish," διδακτός "taught" and ἀμαθία "lack of learning" belong to the same semantic field.[20]

The doctrine of divine education is coherent both as an intellectual construct and as a rule of faith. Life is difficult for the chosen people. Any misstep may lead to divine punishment. But such punishments are never to be deplored or rejected: they are opportunities for bettering oneself. The justification of God's judgments is a frequent motif in Sol.[21]

As in the case of Messianism, the innovative doctrine is conspicuously derived from biblical models.[22]

- It is first introduced in 3:4 in an allusion to Prov 3:11: "the righteous one does not despise being educated by God." This means that

18 Patrick Pouchelle, *Dieu éducateur : Une nouvelle approche d'un concept de la théologie biblique entre Bible Hébraïque, Septante et littérature grecque classique*, FAT II 77 (Tübingen: Mohr Siebeck, 2015).

19 Whether this merely reflects the "habitus" of the authors, as Werline has argued, is to my mind uncertain. Although the authors were scribes, they could develop ideas that had wider currency in the community to which they addressed themselves. See Rodney A. Werline, "The Psalms of Solomon and the Ideology of Rule," in *Conflicted Boundaries in Wisdom and Apocalypticism*, ed. Benjamin G. Wright III, Lawrence M. Wills; SBLSymS 35 (Atlanta: SBL, 2005), 69–87.

20 See Patrick Pouchelle, "Prayers for being disciplined: Notes on παιδεύω and παιδεία in the Psalms of Solomon," in *The Psalms of Solomon: Language, History, Theology, Proceedings of the First International Meeting on the Psalms of Solomon, Strasbourg June 17–18, 2013*, ed. E. Bons, P. Pouchelle, EJL 40 (Atlanta: SBL, 2015), 115–132.

21 See Sol 2:10, 15, 18; 3:5; 4:8; 5:1; 8:7, 8, 23, 26; 9:2; 10:5.

22 As noted by Pouchelle, "Prayers."

failure and hardship are to be welcomed because they are meant to keep the righteous on the straight path.
- The theme is next mentioned in 7:3 in what is probably to be regarded as an allusion to Hos 10:10: "educate us in your will." In context, this amounts to a plea not to let foreign nations have their way with the community. Foreign nations are instruments of chastisement, but God is ultimately in control of everything that happens to Israel, and to the righteous in particular.
- The next Psalm has the statement: "you are our educator"[23] (8:29), which arguably alludes to Hos 5:2, where God is quoted as saying: "I am your educator (παιδευτής)."[24]

Far from stressing the novelty of their views, the authors present the new conception as a scriptural one. In fact, they suggest, nothing is new in their theology, everything they believe and confess flows effortlessly from scripture.[25]

A third theme that may be mentioned in this regard is that of hypocrisy. The distinction between the community to which the authors belong and the group they consider outsiders does not, as in the case of the Qumran scrolls, stem from different versions of religious law. Instead it is a matter of the heart: the rules are the same for everyone, but some observe them sincerely whereas others do not. The authors direct their harshest criticisms against contemporaries who profess piety and observance while secretly transgressing divine laws.[26] As in the case of messianism and divine education, the notion of hypocrisy is not a complete *novum* in Sol. Several passages in the

23 NETS: "you are the one who disciplines us."

24 NETS: "I am one that disciplines you."

25 Testifying to the rhetorical prowess of the authors, Zurawski has recently argued that the concept of divine education in the Psalms of Solomon is simply that of the Hebrew Bible, see Jason Zurawski, "Solomonic Paideia: Divine Pedagogy in the Psalms of Solomon and the Book of Wisdom," in *The Psalms of Solomon: Collected Essays*, ed. Felix Albrecht, Kenneth Atkinson, Patrick Pouchelle, Parabiblica 1 (Tübingen: Mohr Siebeck, 2023), 85–100. This seems to me, however, seriously to undersell the authors' intellectual achievement. Although many elements are indeed attested in the Hebrew Bible, the whole in the Psalms of Solomon is much more than those earlier parts.

26 The motif of secret transgressions is surprisingly frequent in the corpus, see, e.g., Sol 1:7; 4:5, 7; 2:16-17; 8:8, 9.

prophetic books and Psalms do criticize those who under the guise of religiosity fail to live up to God's demands. "With their lips they honor me, but they have removed their heart far from me," Isa 29:13 (cf. Hos 6:6; Am 5:21-24; Isa 1:2-17; Mic 6:5-8; Ps 50/49:22-23; 55/54:22; 78/77:36-37). But the theme is more conspicuous and more elaborate in the Psalms of Solomon than in any part of the Hebrew Bible.[27] What is merely one thread among others in Psalms and prophets becomes a full-blown topic. An entire unit, Sol 4, is devoted to it. There is also a hardening of the notion itself: whereas the prophets engage their people and try to lead them to a more sincere form of worship, the authors conceive of the hypocrites as a group. Hypocrisy is not merely a type of behavior, it is an identity.

In spite of its relative novelty, the way the theme is introduced in Sol 4 strongly foregrounds its scriptural warrant.

- The first verse, Sol 4:1 "Why do you sit, profaner, in the council of the devout, and your heart is far removed from the Lord," defines the theme, with a wink at Isa 29:13, though without using the same vocabulary.
- More prominent is the way the author exploits Psalm 53/52:6 and the word ἀνθρωπάρεσκοι "pleasers of human beings" he found there. The word first occurs in the title of Sol 4. Next, in verses 7 and 8, its meaning, which may not have been clear to all, is defined. Note particularly verse 8: "the man-pleaser who *speaks the law with deceit.*" A "man-pleaser," according to this verse, is a hypocrite.
- Only then does the author insert the explicit allusion to Psalm 53/52:6 in verse 19: "May the flesh of the men-pleasers be scattered by wild beasts."

Alongside the scriptural elements, the author of Sol 4 also uses the verb ὑποκρίνομαι and the noun ὑπόκρισις to express the notion of hypocrisy.[28] This vocabulary had the advantage of clarity. From a background in theatre, where it denoted role play, the word group

27 See Patrick Pouchelle, "Flatterers, Whisperers, and Other Hypocrites: New Denominations for Sinners in the Writings of the Second Temple Period," in *New Vistas on Early Judaism and Christianity: From Enoch to Montréal and Back*, ed. L. DiTommaso, G. Oegema (London: Bloomsbury, 2016), 234–250.

28 See Sol 4:6, 20, 22.

came to express notions of dissimulation and feigning.[29] In Hellenistic Judaism, it was used specifically of religious hypocrisy of the type defined above.[30] With this meaning, this vocabulary is found in the Greek version of Ben Sira, which precedes the Psalms of Solomon.[31] This sporadic attestation could not serve the purpose of anchoring the discourse in scripture.[32] The author prefers to develop his vision of the hypocrites and their destiny on the basis of a somewhat isolated and not entirely clear verse from Psalms.

In elaborating their own views the authors take a selective approach to scripture. They are more sensitive to some themes and tendencies than to others. Their biblical theology is one-sided. They do not usually counter-read scripture. If their reading of scripture is tendentious at all it is in the way they spiritualize the meaning of their intertexts. This can be seen for instance in passages where cultic processes are projected onto individual piety: propitiation is obtained not by sacrifice, but fasting (Sol 3:8); first-fruits are brought not from the field, but the lips (Sol 15:3). Worship is internalized. An additional illustration of this process can be drawn from the allusion to Deut 7:7:

> Sol 4:3
> And his hand is the first upon him as if in zeal,
> and he himself is guilty of various sins and self-indulgence.

In Deuteronomy, the requirement that witnesses in a capital case should throw the first stone is a practical matter, with perhaps a subtext of inculcating collective responsibility. By mentioning the guilt of the witness, the author of Sol 4 brings in a whole new dimension: in order to be able to carry out the divine requirement, witnesses should themselves be blameless. This was not a concern in Deut 17:7. From an instrument regulating public life, the law is turned into a rule of personal sanctification. We are closer to John 8:7—"Let the one among you who

29 For the history of the Greek word group, see Ceslas Spicq, *Theological Lexicon of the New Testament,* Volume 3 (Peabody MA: Hendrickson, 1994), 406–413.
30 See notably Matt 23.
31 Sir 32:15; 33:2.
32 Whether the author of Psalms of Solomon knew the book of Ben Sira is hard to say. As far as I know, there are no definite allusions of the type enumerated in chapter 1.

is without sin be the first to throw a stone"—than to Deuteronomic legislation.

Again it would be possible to add examples of the use of scriptural allusions in Sol's argumentation.[33] But the ones offered here illustrate the intertextual dynamics of this type well enough.

## 2.4. The Psalms of Solomon and the book of Psalms

The literary project of the authors encompasses extending scripture, applying it to their own situation and experience, and making it the basis of their worldview. But an additional aspect of Sol's use of scripture remains to be pointed out. For the authors and their community, scripture is not only *about them*, but also *of them*. Writing in a scriptural vein about contemporary events assimilates them to the authors of scripture.[34] They participate in the continual development of scripture, extending its relevance and hegemony through time.

Here too, marked allusions play an important part. A key exhibit showing the stance of the authors is the following series of allusions to verses from Psalms formulated in the first person:

> **Sol 5:2**
> when I cry out to you, do not pass me by in silence
>
> Psalm 28/27:1
> To you, O Lord, I cried, my God, do not pass me by in silence
>
> **Sol 15:1**
> When I was in distress, I called upon the name of the Lord
>
> Psalm 17:7
> And when I was being afflicted, I called upon the Lord
>
> **Sol 16:1**
> When my soul slumbered, away from the Lord, I slipped for a short time

33 For instance, in Sol 7:6, Ezek 43:7 is alluded to in order to argue that God dwells among the Israelites, not a place; Sol 9:2 refers to Deut 28:25 to show that the diaspora is part of God's plan.

34 Compare, *mutatis mutandis*, the foundational work of Hindy Najman, *Seconding Sinai: The Development of Mosaic Discourse in Second Temple Judaism*, JSJS 77 (Leiden: Brill, 2003).

Psalm 119/118:28
My soul slumbered from exhaustion[35]

**Sol 16:9**
Direct the works of my hands in your place

Psalm 90/89:17
Direct upon us the work of our hand

**Sol 17:1**
In you, O God, shall our soul boast

Psalm 34/33:3
In the Lord my soul shall boast

As will be appreciated, the allusions preserve the first-person formulation of the verses alluded to, notwithstanding variations between singular and plural in the last two examples. At first blush, this intertextual procedure may appear to efface the speakers of the Psalms verse and to install the authors in their stead. This is hardly the right way of putting it, however. The authors of the Psalms of Solomon are not into appropriation—remember that they remain studiously anonymous. It would be more correct to say they efface their own identity so as to impersonate scriptural authors. Even better would be to view the process as one of identification: the authors recognize themselves in the human voices one hears in Psalms.

Arguably, the biblical Psalms were created with the express view to making some type of identification possible. Enemies are rarely named in the Psalms, nor diseases described in detail. Sins, too, are generally defined in a way that leaves much latitude for the reader to find an image of him- or herself in the text of the Psalm. The literary move we see in the Psalms of Solomon goes further, however. The authors do not recognize themselves only in the ordeals of the Psalmists, but also in the way the Psalmists managed to speak out. The authors intend to give an authoritative voice to their experience in the same way as do the Psalmists.

For the understanding of Psalms of Solomon these observations are crucial. They give coherence to the entire use of scripture manifest in the corpus. The principle of identification accounts for the poetic form of the Psalms of Solomon. It also explains the use of special vocabulary reviewed in section 2.1: "creation," "law," "covenant,"

35 English translations slightly modified to bring out the similarity.

"atonement," "blessing," etc. Although these terms are strewn over a wide range of writings, as a group they are exhaustively refracted in Psalms specifically. The same principle provides the authors with a stylistic format to treat biblical themes: the Psalms do not usually refer expressly to earlier texts,[36] but instead freely recreate existing stories and motifs in their own discourse. Uniting historical narratives, prophetic preaching, wisdom motifs and religious parenesis into a single literary genre, the Psalms are like a miniature of scripture.[37] A similar mode of representation is found in the Psalms of Solomon.

A final aspect of the authorial stance we observe in Psalms of Solomon still needs to be underscored: not only do they recognize themselves in the Psalmists as sufferers and as speakers, but as writers as well. The Psalms of Solomon are stylized in imitation of the biblical Psalms. Particularly telling is the use of the term διάψαλμα, the standard rendering of Hebrew סֶלָה, in Sol 17:29 and 18:9,[38] and, even more so, the titles, which loosely follow the format of the titles in Psalms.

## 2.5. Solomon in the Psalms of Solomon

All songs except the first one have a title.[39] Many titles contain a hint (not always particularly helpful) as to the contents of the song.[40] Some titles provide information on the genre and the musical quality of the songs: "psalm" occurs six times, "hymn" in Sol 14 and 16, "with

36 Exceptions occur in some of the titles, e.g. Psalm 51/50:2; 52/51:2; 54/53:2.

37 So Martin Luther in his introduction to the Psalter (Zweiter Vorrede auf den Psalter, 1528): "(The Psalter) could well be entitled a 'Little Bible' since everything contained in the entire Bible is beautifully and briefly comprehended, and compacted into a Manual" ("Das es wol möcht ein kleine Biblia heissen darin alles auffs schönest vnd kürtzest so in der gantzen Biblia stehet gefasset vnd zu einem feinen Enchiridion oder Handbuch gemacht vnd bereitet ist").

38 The term διάψαλμα is found also in Hab 3:3, 9, 13, assimilating Hab 3 to a Psalm.

39 Note, however, that in Albrecht's edition, Sol 1 does have a title (for the text-critical basis of this decision, see Albrecht, *Psalmi Salomonis*, 54).

40 Sol 2 "about Jerusalem," Sol 3 "about the righteous," Sol 4 "pertaining to the men-pleasers," Sol 6 "in hope," Sol 7 "of returning," Sol 9 "for rebuke," Sol 11 "for expectation," Sol 13 "against the tongue of the lawless," Sol 16 "for help of the devout," Sol 17 "for the king."

an ode" in Sol 15 and 17,[41] and "among hymns" in Sol 10.[42] All these elements echo elements in the titles of Psalms.

In addition, every title contains an ascription to Solomon: τῷ Σαλωμων "pertaining to Solomon," and once, in Sol 4, τοῦ Σαλωμων "of Solomon." Many commentators have held that the attribution to Solomon is secondary, because the songs "do not hint at any connection with Solomon and the circumstances in which he reigned."[43] The premise is correct, but the corollary does not follow. A closer look makes the secondary nature of the ascriptions unlikely.[44] The wording of the attribution parallels the format in Psalms, in most cases precisely. There are two main formats:

> "Pertaining to Solomon" (τῷ Σαλωμων), Sol 6–13
> Compare: "Pertaining to David" (τῷ Δαυιδ), Psalm 32/31; 33/32; 34/33; 35/34, etc.
>
> "A Psalm. Pertaining to Solomon (Ψαλμὸς τῷ Σαλωμων), Sol 2, 3, 5, 15, 17, 18
> Compare: "A Psalm. Pertaining to David" (Ψαλμὸς τῷ Δαυιδ), Psalm 3; 94/93; 98/97; 99/98, etc.

In some cases only partially:

> "Dialogue of Solomon" (Διαλογὴ τοῦ Σαλωμων), Sol 4
> Compare: "Prayer of David" (Προσευχὴ τοῦ Δαυιδ), Psalm 17/16:1
> "A Hymn. Pertaining to Solomon" (Ὕμνος τῷ Σαλωμων), Sol 14, 16
> Compare: "the hymns of David have ended" (Ἐξέλιπον οἱ ὕμνοι Δαυιδ), Psalm 72/71:20

It is hard to imagine that the variety of attributions, closely corresponding to similar variety in Psalms, came about by incremental scribal accretion. Moreover, the immediate effect of the analogy tallies

41 This expression is not attested in Psalms, but it is found in the title of Hab 3:1.

42 In the Septuagint of Psalms, ἐν ὕμνοις is the equivalent of בִּנְגִינוֹת (e.g. Psalm 6:1). See also in chapter 4 the discussion of εἰς νῖκος in the title of Sol 8.

43 For a recent review of the history of research on this question, see Gordley, "Psalms of Solomon as Solomonic Discourse," 54–56.

44 The titles are missing in the Syriac version of the Psalms of Solomon, but the significance of this fact is hard to evaluate. The titles may well have been omitted by the Syriac translator, or at some stage in the transmission of the Syriac version.

with several other characteristics pointed out in the present chapter: it assimilates the editorial form of Psalms of Solomon to that of Psalms. The Psalms of Solomon seriously pretend to be a writing of the same type as the biblical Psalms. This literary strategy underlies much of the style and content matter of the corpus. We may conclude that the array of titles, including the ascriptions, reflects authorial planning and goes back to an early stage in the production of the corpus.

But why Solomon? This is not an easy question. The ascriptions suggest that the role of Solomon in the collection corresponds to that of David in the Psalms. Thus the parallel shows that king Solomon, son of David, is meant. As an extension of scripture, the Psalms of Solomon are not equivalent to Psalms, but they are intimately related—the way Solomon is related to David.

The dative case is not commonly used in Greek to express authorship—NETS systematically translates as "pertaining to." Even so, the occasional use of the genitive, in both Psalms and Psalms of Solomon, shows that the notion of authorship remains relevant.[45] Various notices, in scripture and other Jewish writings, confirm that both David and Solomon were known for composing songs.[46]

Beyond this we can only speculate. It is easier to eliminate false leads than to identify the correct implication. Solomon commonly stands for wisdom of various sorts,[47] but this aspect can hardly account for the ascriptions, for Psalms of Solomon is not a wisdom writing.[48] And although Solomon is also the builder of the Jerusalem temple,[49]

45 See Albert Pietersma, "David in the Greek Psalms," *VT* 30 (1980), 213–226; Gilles Dorival, "Autour des Titres des Psaumes," *RevSR* 73 (1999), 165–176. Perhaps the use of the dative invites the reader to take the notion of authorship with a grain of salt.

46 Solomon is said to have composed songs (1 Kgs 5:12 [4:32]: "his songs were a thousand and five"), and Psalms 72/71 and 127/126, as well as Song of Songs, are attributed to him. However, whereas those three poems do contain potential references to Solomon, in our corpus the authors speak from their own point of view and never impersonate Solomon.

47 See notably the books of Proverbs, Ecclesiastes and Wisdom of Solomon, as well as Ben Sira in the Old Latin version.

48 For discussion, see Pouchelle, "The Simple Bare Necessities."

49 Psalm 127/126 was probably attributed to Solomon because of this trait.

the way the temple is mentioned in the Psalms of Solomon hardly invites a reference to its builder.[50]

The one song that lends itself to association with Solomon is Sol 17. The Messianic figure who will inaugurate a new era is to be a "son of David" (17:21). His wisdom is underscored repeatedly (17:23, 29, 35). He will judge his people and the nations (17:26, 19). He will also "bless the people of the Lord" (17:35). These traits do indeed remind one of Solomon as presented in Kings and Chronicles.[51] Some commentators think the attribution to Solomon was first attracted by Sol 17 and spread from there to the rest of the corpus.[52]

We should not, however, overlook a few anti-Solomonic traits that occur in the description of the Messiah: he will not multiply horses, nor gold and silver (17:33); he will rule over his flock in equity, without oppressing anyone (17:41). These indications do not agree with what is told in the historical books. Instead, as was pointed out in section 2.3, they assimilate the Messiah to the authors and intended readers of the corpus. The Messiah, according to 17:33, will not multiply riches, just as the pious too are encouraged to be content with what God gives them:

> **Sol 5:16**
> Happy is the man whom God remembers in due proportion
> to sufficiency,
> If man has too much, he sins.

In 17:32 it is said that the future king will be "taught by God" (διδακτὸς ὑπὸ θεοῦ), a quality that suits the pious as those whom God educates (see above in section 2.3). According to 17:27 the king "shall not allow injustice to lodge" in the midst of the people, which echoes 3:6–7, "in the house of the righteous sin upon sin does not lodge." Finally, one will note that the rule of the Messiah is described predominantly in terms of speech acts: he will threaten and reprove (17:25), judge (17:26, 29, 43), glorify (17:30), bless (17:35), rebuke (17:36); he will "strike the earth with the word of his mouth" (17:35, cf. v. 36b), "his words will be more refined than costly gold," they are "as words of the holy" (17:43). Some of these statements assimilate his

50 As argued, unpersuasively, by Gordley, "Psalms of Solomon as Solomonic Discourse," 71 and passim.

51 See 1 Kgs 3:28 (judging); 1 Kgs 8:14; 2 Chron 6:3 (blessing)

52 See notably Ryle and James, *Psalms of Pharisees*, lxi.

actions to those of God, but the great stress on discursive acts puts the Messiah on one line with the pious ones: they bless (2:33; 3:1; 6:4), justify (4:8), confess (10:6), praise (10:7). They do very little else:

> **Sol 15:2–3**
> For who, O God, is strong except to confess to you in truth?
> And wherein is a person mighty except in confessing to your name?
> A new melody with an ode in gladness of heart,
> the fruit of the lips with the tuned instrument of the tongue,
> the first fruit of the lips from a devout and righteous heart.

Power belongs to God. All the human being can do is to respond to God's mighty acts through speech. This is as true for the community of readers as for the royal figure described in Sol 17.

What all this means is that we should read Sol 17 in light of the entire corpus rather than the other way round. The Solomonic figure of Sol 17 did not lend his name to the other songs, but whatever is Solomonic in the character of the pious "rubbed off" on the Messiah of Sol 17. What, then, is the meaning of the name Solomon? After having eliminated all the other possibilities the sole remaining notion is that of filiation. In his capacity as son of David, Solomon represents the ambition of the authors to write psalms like those of David. They do not pretend to be David, but son of David—the composer of Psalms. The fact that Solomon too was known as a composer of songs enhanced the suggestion, but the main implication was the relation to David.

However this may be, the "scripture-like" quality of the titles in Psalms of Solomon are beyond doubt. The editors of the corpus, who were working on the same lines as the authors, and may belong to the same group, intended to create a written corpus modeled on Psalms.

## 2.6. Conclusions

The literary procedures described in the preceding sections partly overlap. They are not meant as neat categories into which to pigeonhole individual passages. Rather than to establish categories of scriptural allusion, I have tried to look at various aspects of the intertextual poetics of Psalms of Solomon. In the end what emerges is a rather coherent mode of literary representation closely following the model of the book of Psalms.

# 3.
# Psalms of Solomon's Text of Scripture: The Septuagint

The question at the heart of the present study is which text of scripture the authors of the Psalms of Solomon were using. Was it an oral tradition or a written text? Was it a single edition or did they consult various versions? In which language did they read their scriptures, and which text type did they know?

## 3.1. Distinguishing scriptural from non-scriptural elements

The survey in chapter 2 may suggest that such questions cannot be answered. The authors of the Psalms of Solomon select their scriptural references, mix them with other elements, and manipulate them to express their own ideas. In light of these processes, one may wonder whether any text-historical analysis of the allusions is possible. How can we distinguish the scriptural text from the interpretation the author adds to it?

In fact, however, it is precisely the Psalms of Solomon's dynamics of intertextuality that make this distinction possible. Let us consider an example:

> Sol 3:8
> **ἐξιλάσατο περὶ ἀγνοίας** ἐν νηστείᾳ καὶ ταπεινώσει ψυχῆς αὐτοῦ
> he made atonement for sins of ignorance by fasting and humiliation of his soul

> Lev 5:18
> καὶ **ἐξιλάσεται** περὶ αὐτοῦ ὁ ἱερεὺς **περὶ** τῆς **ἀγνοίας** αὐτοῦ
> and the priest shall make atonement for him concerning his ignorance

In chapter 2 we saw that the authors of the Psalms of Solomon are at pains to anchor their assertions in scripture, even if what they say goes beyond what they found there. Sol 3:8 is a parade example of this procedure. While harking back to Lev 5:18, as argued in chapter 1, the point the author seeks to make is different from that of the proof text. The key novelty in this instance is that atonement is not obtained by means of an offering, as in Lev 5, but by practises of personal piety. Non-sacrificial reparation is an important theme in the Psalms of Solomon.[1] Alongside fasting, prayer (Sol 6:1), almsgiving (Sol 9:5), confession of sins (Sol 9:6) and suffering (Sol 10:1–2; 12:10; 13:5) are named as salvatory processes.[2] Note also, that the priest effects atonement in Leviticus, whereas the righteous do so for themselves in the Psalms of Solomon.

The expression ἐξιλάσατο περὶ ἀγνοίας "he atoned for (sins of) ignorance," which recalls Leviticus, does the anchoring, but the novel idea is elaborated in words that do not echo the prooftext. The part that reflects scripture is meant to be recognized as such, so as to provide justification for the entire sentence.

The duality illustrated in this example is found in many scriptural allusions of the Psalms of Solomon. A typical allusion combines sufficient faithfulness to the scriptural source text with necessary divergences to adapt the thought to the new context.[3]

## 3.2. The Septuagint as intertext

What immediately stands out when one lists the substantial allusions to scripture in the Psalms of Solomon—as we did in chapter 1—is the prominence of Septuagintal elements. Although we encounter a small number of allusions that do not reflect the Septuagint, or not strongly,

1 See Arnaldo Momigliano, "Religion in Athens, Rome, and Jerusalem in the First Century B.C.," in idem *On Pagans, Jews, and Christians* (Middletown CT: Wesleyan University Press, 1987), 74–91, in particular 80–82.

2 Note also the expression ἀπαρχὴ χειλέων "first-fruits of the lips" (Sol 15:3), which transposes an institution of the temple cult into the sphere of personal piety.

3 For a more detailed analysis of some of the techniques the authors use in transforming fragments of scripture, see Patrick Pouchelle, "Les scribes à l'œuvre dans les Psaumes de Salomon," *Henoch* 42 (2020), 344–359.

the general tendency is for "the part that reflects scripture" to conform to the Greek version.

Allusions aligning with the Septuagint: 1:3; 2:8, 12, 17, 18, 20; 3:2, 4, 8, 10, 12; 4:3, 19, 20; 5:2, 5, 19; 7:6; 8:2, 9, 14a, 14b; 9:2; 10:2; 11:1, 2; 12:6; 13:5; 15:1, 3, 4, 5, 6; 16:1, 9; 17:7, 15, 21, 27, 30, 33, 35 (41 cases)

Allusions LXX aligning partly with the MT against the Septuagint: 5:3; 7:3; 9:9; 11:7; 16:2; 17:1, 3, 23–24 (8 cases)

The present chapter will focus on the first group, the second group will be analyzed in more detail in chapter 4.

By itself, the agreement between the allusions and the Septuagint gives no immediate purchase on our questions. Various scenarios could account for the conformity of the allusions to the Greek version. To the extent they have given any thought to these questions, most scholars have set out from the notion that the Psalms of Solomon were created in Hebrew. This would imply that the conformity with the Septuagint does not go back to the original writing but reflects the work of a translator of the Psalms of Solomon. This is perfectly possible, at least in theory. To begin with, the conformity could simply be attributed to the fact that the Psalms of Solomon are preserved in Greek. When they were translated from the Hebrew, the translation of the allusions would naturally have turned out to be close to the Septuagint.

This explanation might fairly be applied to some of the Psalms of Solomon's allusions.[4] It could not, however, account for the rather consistent alignment of the allusions with the Septuagint. Language is a flexible instrument and there are almost always various ways to express a given thought. Moral or theological truths of the type we find in the Psalms of Solomon would be particularly amenable to different ways of putting them into Greek. There is no reason why, in 41 out of 49 cases, the translation of the Psalms of Solomon should agree with the Septuagint by mere accident.

Moreover, in several instances, the diction of the allusion is to some extent distinctive, thus making accidental correspondence unlikely:

> **Sol 3:4**
> οὐκ **ὀλιγωρήσει** δίκαιος **παιδευόμενος** ὑπὸ **κυρίου**
> The righteous does not despise being disciplined by the Lord

4 See for instance 2:17, 20; 3:8, 12; 5:19; 7:3; 9:9; 11:7; 15:6, 9; 16:9; 17:1, 3, 7, 17–18, 33.

Prov 3:11
Υἱέ, μὴ **ὀλιγώρει παιδείας κυρίου**
My son, do not belittle the Lord's discipline
מוּסַר יְהוָה בְּנִי אַל־תִּמְאָס
My child, do not despise the LORD's discipline

It is doubtful whether the translator of Sol 3 would have used the rare verb ὀλιγωρέω if it weren't for the Greek version of the text alluded to. In the entire Septuagint, Prov 3:11 is the only passage where this Greek verb is used to translate the verb מאס "to despise." The rendering is faithful enough, but it is also distinctive.[5]

Within the "Hebrew approach," scholars have therefore reached for a more powerful explanation of the phenomenon. In this explanation, the constant agreement of the allusions with the Septuagint text is not due to mere chance. Instead it indicates that the translator of the Hebrew Psalms of Solomon consciously or semi-consciously conformed scriptural allusions to the Septuagint version, with which he was intimately familiar. An explicit statement of Viteau merits to be quoted here:

> The translator of the Psalms of Solomon was a Hellenizing Jew; he knew the Septuagint perfectly [...]. While translating the Psalms of Solomon, he was constantly influenced by the Greek Bible, for, firstly, the ideas he needed to express had already received their Greek form there, and, secondly, the habit of reading the Septuagint constantly provided his pen with expressions and constructions from the Old Testament. Similarities between the Septuagint version and the version of the Psalms of Solomon were therefore inevitable.[6]

5 Other examples of distinct formulations that would hardly be reproduced accidentally are found in 1:3; 3:10; 4:3, 20; 5:2, 3; 8:2, 14a; 10:2; 11:1; 13:5; 16:1; 17:27.

6 Joseph Viteau, *Les Psaumes de Salomon* (Paris: Letouzey & Ané, 1911), 123: "Le traducteur des Psaumes de Salomon était un Juif hellénisant; il connaissait parfaitement les Septante, non seulement les livres proto-canoniques, mais encore les livres deutéro-canoniques, qui n'existaient qu'en grec et n'étaient lus que par les Juifs hellénisants. En traduisant les Psaumes de Salomon, il était constamment soumis à l'influence de la Bible grecque ; car d'un côté, les idées à rendre y avaient déjà reçu leur forme grecque ; de l'autre côté, l'habitude de lire les Septante fournissait constamment à sa plume les expressions et les constructions de la version

In this passage, Viteau is not focusing exclusively on scriptural allusions. Nevertheless, an explanation along the lines he lays down may indeed account for many more instances of scriptural allusion in the Psalms of Solomon.

However, even this more sophisticated approach cannot account for all of the Psalms of Solomon's allusions. Several scriptural references in the Psalms of Solomon involve passages for which the Septuagint version diverges from the Hebrew. As will be shown in the following sections, such examples raise serious objections to the "Hebrew approach," even in the version spelled out by Viteau.

A third explanation must therefore be considered: the authors of the Psalms of Solomon wrote the text in Greek, in reference to Greek intertexts; the allusions that involve features of the Septuagint go back to the original writing. This approach will account for the entire set of scriptural allusions in the Psalms of Solomon.

## 3.3. Allusions to divergent Septuagint passages

In several passages alluded to in the Psalms of Solomon, the Septuagint text underlying the allusion diverges from the Hebrew. The divergence may be due to free interpretation:

**Sol 17:35**
πατάξει γὰρ γῆν **τῷ λόγῳ** τοῦ στόματος αὐτοῦ εἰς αἰῶνα
For he shall strike the earth with the word of his mouth forever

Isa 11:4
καὶ πατάξει γῆν **τῷ λόγῳ** τοῦ στόματος αὐτοῦ
And he shall strike the earth with the word of his mouth
וְהִכָּה־אֶרֶץ **בְּשֵׁבֶט** פִּיו
And he shall strike the earth with the rod of his mouth.

As was pointed out in chapter 1, the "rod of his mouth" of the MT becomes the "word of his mouth" in the Septuagint. Although it is impossible to rule out that the Septuagint reflects a different source text, the most likely explanation in this case is that the variant was created by the Greek translator of Isaiah. Realizing that the rod was

de l'Ancien Testament. Les ressemblances entre la version des Septante et la version des Psaumes de Salomon étaient donc inévitables."

used as a figure of speech, he decided to decode the metaphor. The allusion in Sol 17:35 conforms to the Septuagint version of Isa 11:4.

Additional passages alluded to where MT and Septuagint diverge due to free translation include the following:

- in Isa 59:2, alluded to in 2:8, God turns away from his people in the Septuagint while the people's sin is the subject of the verb in the Hebrew; the Greek text also refers to "pitying" explicitly and not to mere "hearing" as does the Masoretic Text;
- in Num 25:4, alluded to in 2:12, παραδειγματίζω "to make a show of" is a contextual interpretation of Hebrew הוקיע "to impale, to hang, to expose with broken limbs";
- in Psalm 53/52:6, alluded to in 4:19, ἀνθρωπάρεσκος "pleaser of humans" seems to be a guess, poorly capturing the meaning of the Hebrew חֹנָךְ "the one who camps against you."[7]

Other divergences between the Hebrew and Greek versions of the Psalms of Solomon intertext appear to reflect variant readings rather than interpretation:

**Sol 7:6**
Ἐν τῷ κατασκηνοῦν **τὸ ὄνομά σου** ἐν μέσῳ ἡμῶν ἐλεηθησόμεθα
While your name dwells in our midst, we shall find pity

Ezek 43:7
ἐν οἷς κατασκηνώσει **τὸ ὄνομά μου** ἐν μέσῳ οἴκου Ισραηλ τὸν αἰῶνα
in which my name shall encamp in the midst of the house of Israel forever

אֲשֶׁר אֶשְׁכָּן־**שָׁם** בְּתוֹךְ בְּנֵי־יִשְׂרָאֵל לְעוֹלָם
where I will reside among the people of Israel forever.

---

7 It has been mooted that the Greek rendering reflects a variant reading חנף (see BHS), or that the translator interpreted the received Hebrew in light of the root חנן, see Pouchelle, "ἀνθρωπάρεσκος," *HTLS*. Another possibility is that the translator of Psalms was thinking of Henoch (חֲנוֹךְ), who according to Midrash Genesis Rabba 25 was a hypocrite, see J. Theodor, Ch. Albeck, *Midrash Bereshit Rabba. Critical Edition with Notes and Commentary* (Jerusalem: Shalem, 1996 [first edition published in Berlin, 1912-1937), 238. This midrashic notion may have been known already in Second-Temple times.

Instead of שָׁם "there," the Septuagint attests the reading שֵׁם "name" (or שְׁמִי "my name"). The allusion in Sol 7:6 follows the Septuagint.[8]

Again, there are several other examples that exhibit a similar profile:

- in 8:9, the allusion to Ezek 22:6 reflects the Septuagint version, which is based on a variant reading: זֶרַע "seed," for MT's זְרֹעַ "arm";
- in 8:14b, the allusion to Jer 25/32:15 reflects a variant reading, חמר "wine" (LXX ἄκρατος "unmixed") instead of MT's חמה "fury";[9] admittedly, this variant may only have existed in the mind of the translator of Jeremiah;[10]
- in 17:15, the allusion to Ezek 30:5 rests on a shorter reading, בני ברית "sons of the covenant" (LXX τῶν υἱῶν τῆς διαθήκης), for MT's בְּנֵי אֶרֶץ הַבְּרִית.

In all these cases, the Greek text of the Psalms of Solomon goes with the Septuagint.

How can we account for the fact that the allusions in the Psalms of Solomon follow the Septuagint version in cases like this? On the supposition that the Psalms of Solomon were created as a Hebrew text, one would have to submit that the translators identified the intertexts, looked them up in the Septuagint version—or knew them by heart—and adopted the Septuagint variants in their own translation of the Psalms of Solomon. The translators would in effect be giving greater authority to the text of the Septuagint than to their own source text—not to speak of the received Hebrew text of scripture. Such a scenario is not unthinkable. The translators of the Psalms of Solomon may have adopted the Septuagintal variants so as to enable their readers to identify the allusion. They may have intended the Greek translation of the Psalms of Solomon to be read together with the Greek writings that in time would come to make up the Septuagint. In that case, they would naturally have made sure that the text of the allusion agreed with the Greek version of the intertext. As we will see in section 3.5, this procedure has precedent.

---

8 The syntax of Ezek 43:7 is not favorable to the Septuagint's reading, and the notion of "making the name to dwell" is otherwise unattested in Ezekiel. The Septuagint reading reflects the influence of Deuteronomy (see Deut 12:11; Jer 7:12).

9 Cf. Psalm 75/74:9.

10 Note that the gender of the demonstrative adjective הַזֹּאת does not agree with חמר, as read by the translator, but with חמה, as in the MT.

Nevertheless, an obstacle remains to the "Hebrew approach." Once an allusion such as the ones discussed in the present section existed, its Septuagint form might be explained along the lines suggested above. But the "Hebrew approach" cannot, at least not in every instance, account for the creation of these allusions in the first place.

## 3.4. Fruitful variants

A crucial observation on allusions involving divergent passages in the Septuagint is that some of them appear to be central to the literary strategy of the author of the Psalms of Solomon:

> **Sol 2:12**
> ἀπέναντι τοῦ ἡλίου παρεδειγμάτισαν ἀδικίας αὐτῶν.
> before the sun they paraded their injustices
>
> Num 25:4
> καὶ παραδειγμάτισον αὐτοὺς κυρίῳ ἀπέναντι τοῦ ἡλίου
> and make an example of them to the Lord before the sun
> וְהוֹקַע אוֹתָם לַיהוָה נֶגֶד הַשָּׁמֶשׁ
> and impale them in the sun before the LORD

While the Septuagint version of Num 25:4 is defensible in the context of Num 25, παραδειγματίζω and הוקיע are not synonyms. The Greek verb foregrounds public shaming, while the Hebrew verb refers strictly to the mechanics of the execution.

In the context of Sol 2, only the meaning of the Greek verb is relevant. The rich analogies between the sin of Baal Peor and Pompey's occupation of Jerusalem (see chapter 2) crystallize in the use of the Greek verb. The Romans had enslaved those Jerusalemites who had opposed them and paraded them for all to see. The entire point of the allusion is tied to the wording of the Septuagint. Note also that the Hebrew verb could not have been used with the direct object it has in Sol 2:12—"their sins." The Hebrew verb can only be used with a human direct object. These observations put near-insuperable obstacles in the way of the "Hebrew hypothesis." If Sol 2 were created in Hebrew, the author would not have thought of Num 25:4, and even if he had, there would have been no easy way to reference the intertext. If the Psalm was composed in Hebrew, the allusion to Num 25:4 can hardly be traced back to the author. It could only have been smuggled in by an unusually creative translator.

As against this, the "Greek hypothesis" is fully able to account for the way Num 25:4 is woven into Sol 2. An author steeped in the Septuagint and writing in Greek about the public shaming of Jerusalemite notables could easily have been reminded of the verb παραδειγματίζω in Num 25, and spun out the allusion from there.

**Sol 4:19**
Σκορπισθείησαν σάρκες ἀνθρωπαρέσκων ὑπὸ θηρίων,
καὶ ὀστᾶ παρανόμων κατέναντι τοῦ ἡλίου ἐν ἀτιμίᾳ
May the flesh of the men-pleasers be scattered by wild beasts,
and may the bones of the transgressors of the law lie before the sun in dishonor

In this case again, the scriptural allusion seems to have been triggered by the Greek word used in Psalm 53/52:6. How חֹנָךְ "the one encamping against you" came to be translated as "pleasers of human beings" in Ps 53/52 is not fully understood.[11] What is clear, however, is that the Greek word fitted the purposes of the author of Sol 4:19 very well. The noun ἀνθρωπάρεσκος and the cognate verb are not attested in non-Jewish texts.[12] In Jewish and early Christian literature, they are used systematically in contexts of dissembling and dishonesty.[13] "Pleasers of human beings" are those who practice Jewish law not from the heart, but in order to gain prestige. As we saw in chapter 2, this is also how the author of Sol 4 defined the term. The entire song is about hypocrites, who make a show of abiding by God's law while secretly transgressing both its letter and its spirit.

An author writing in Hebrew would hardly have turned to Psalm 53/52 to strengthen the argument, for in its Hebrew version, the Psalm is not about hypocrisy. Only the Greek version is relevant. These data strongly favor a Greek origin for Sol 4.

**Sol 8:9**
υἱὸς μετὰ μητρὸς καὶ πατὴρ μετὰ θυγατρὸς συνεφύροντο
they committed incest, son with mother and father with daughter

11 See above, note 6.
12 See the exhaustive review in Pouchelle, "ἀνθρωπάρεσκος."
13 See e.g. *Test. Aser* 3.2 (note διπρόσωποι "double-faced" in the near context); Eph 6:6; Col 3:22 (note ὀφθαλμοδουλία "eyeservice" in the contexts).

Here again, only the interpretation found in the Septuagint version of Ezek 22:6 could serve to reinforce the point that one of the crimes of the Jerusalem elites was incest.[14] One might speculate that a similar interpretation of Ezek 22:6 was known in circles who based their exegesis on the Hebrew text—after all, the divergence is a matter of vocalization only. Such a view is built on sand, however. Outside of the Septuagint and its sphere of influence not a hint can be found that the reading "each one to his seed" was ever envisaged in the interpretation of the passage. This instance therefore also strongly favors the Greek hypothesis. An author composing Sol 8 in Hebrew would not have looked to Ezek 22:6 to establish his case.

Allusions to scripture are not mere embellishments in the Psalms of Solomon. As was discussed in chapter 2, they are tools of persuasion, as well as tokens of the authors' world view. If allusions turn out consistently to work better for the rhetoric of the Psalms of Solomon in their Septuagintal form than in Hebrew, this is a strong argument for the hypothesis that the Psalms were created in Greek.

## 3.5. An extended test case

One of the passages identified in chapter 1 allows us to review the "Hebrew" and "Greek" approaches to the allusions contained in the Psalms of Solomon.

In one of the curses contained in Deut 28 we find a striking, and fascinating, divergence between the Hebrew text and the Septuagint:

Deut 28:25

וְהָיִיתָ לְזַעֲוָה לְכֹל מַמְלְכוֹת הָאָרֶץ

You shall become an *object of horror* to all the kingdoms of the earth

LXX

καὶ ἔσῃ ἐν διασπορᾷ ἐν πάσαις ταῖς βασιλείαις τῆς γῆς

And you shall be in *dispersion* in all the kingdoms of the earth

The rendering διασπορά "dispersion" either corresponds to a daring interpretation of MT's זַעֲוָה, or reflects a variant reading, perhaps a form of the root זרע "to sow."[15] In any case, the Greek rendering

14 For the Hebrew and Greek texts of Ezek 22:6, see below in section 3.6.

15 See the next note.

clearly diverges from the meaning of the Hebrew equivalent זועה / זעוה "trembling, terror."[16] The change entailed a rewriting of the entire verse: instead of Israel "becoming an object of terror *to* all the kingdoms," as in the MT, it will "be in dispersion *among* all the kingdoms" in the Septuagint. Thus the idea of dispersion is introduced into a verse that originally spoke only of adversity and shame for Israel. The divergence was surely relevant to the Greek translator of Deuteronomy, who was for all we know a Jew of the diaspora.

Jer 41/34:17
καὶ δώσω ὑμᾶς εἰς διασπορὰν πάσαις ταῖς βασιλείαις τῆς γῆς
I will give you as a *dispersion* to all the kingdoms of the earth.
וְנָתַתִּי אֶתְכֶם לְזַוְעָה לְכֹל מַמְלְכוֹת הָאָרֶץ
I will make you an *object of horror* to all the kingdoms of the earth

In the MT, Jer 34:17 picks up on Deut 28:25. What was predicted in the Torah is now about to become a reality. The meaning of the word זועה / זעוה is the same as before. The translator of Jeremiah renders it as διασπορά, following the Septuagint of Deuteronomy. We may submit that the translator (or corrector) of this part of Jeremiah acted in accordance with what was described above in section 3.4: he identified the reference to Deut 28:25 in the Hebrew text of Jeremiah, looked up the Greek rendering of that verse (or knew it by heart), and borrowed part of it including the word διασπορά even although it

16 The Hebrew word זועה / זעוה, "trembling, terror" is attested eight times in the Hebrew Bible. It is more or less correctly translated in Jer 15:4; Ezek 23:46; 2 Chron 29:8. In Deut 28:25, the divergence between the Hebrew and the Greek may be explained in different ways. The Hebrew may have been misread, or the translator may have wanted to refer to his own situation and that of his audience; perhaps this is a case where one could argue the Hebrew was intentionally misread. The rendering has been much discussed in the literature, but the main question has not been why the translator diverged from the Hebrew, but whether διασπορά in the Greek text has negative connotations, see e.g. Willem C. van Unnik, *Das Selbstverständnis der jüdischen Diaspora in der hellenistisch-römischen Zeit,* aus dem Nachlaß herausgegeben und bearbeitet von Pieter Willem van der Horst (Leiden: Brill, 1993), 91–92, 95. More secondary literature is quoted in *Septuaginta Deutsch. Erläuterungen und Kommentare zum griechischen Alten Testament,* Bd I (Stuttgart: Deutsche Bibelgesellschaft, 2011), 585–586.

neither corresponded to its equivalent in the Hebrew text, nor fitted the context. The notion of dispersion has no more contextual warrant in Jer 34:17 than in Deut 28:25.

The reason for adopting the rendering from Deuteronomy may be that the translator of Jeremiah was unsure of the meaning of Hebrew זעוה / זועה.[17] Beyond this, however, it seems likely that he wished to preserve the allusion in a form that would be recognizable to readers of the Greek scriptures. If they knew that passage in Deuteronomy, or were likely to come across it in their liturgy, they should be able to realize that the verse in Jeremiah referred to it. All of this shows the force of the "Hebrew scenario."

> **Sol. 9:2**
> ἐν παντὶ ἔθνει ἡ διασπορὰ τοῦ Ισραηλ κατὰ τὸ ῥῆμα τοῦ θεοῦ
> Among every nation is Israel's dispersion, according to the word of God

In Sol 9:2, the wording of Deut 28:25 is followed less faithfully, yet the general meaning is the same. The use of the word διασπορά makes it likely that there we are dealing with an allusion. In addition, the expression "according to the word of God" indicates that the Sol 9 is here referring to a biblical passage, and none fits the bill better than Deut 28:25.

On the supposition that the Psalms of Solomon were composed in Hebrew one might try to explain the use of the word διασπορά in Sol 9:2 in the same way as in Jer 41/34:17: the translator of Sol 9:2 recognized the allusion to Deut 28:25, looked up the passage in the Septuagint, and decided to adopt some of its wording to preserve the allusion for a reader knowing no Hebrew. This sounds plausible enough. But it doesn't explain why the author of Sol 9 would have referred to that passage in the first place. The main theme in this part of Sol 9 is Israel's forcible exile far from its own land:

---

17 In Jer 24:9, which also alludes to Deut 28:25, the word זעוה/זועה is rendered with the word διασκορπισμόν "scattering," a near synonym of διασπορά. This is a slender basis, however, for the claim that זעוה/זועה was more generally interpreted to mean "dispersion." What led the translator of this part of Jeremiah to use διασκορπισμόν is most probably not the Hebrew word as such, but the perception that the verse alluded to the Deuteronomic curse.

**Sol 9:1**
When Israel was led away in exile to a foreign land,
when they fell away from the Lord who redeemed them,
they were expelled from the inheritance, which the Lord had given them.

If the Psalm were written in Hebrew, the author would hardly be led to refer to Deut 28:25 at this point, a passage that has nothing to say of exile. Only the Septuagint version, read independently, could serve as a prediction of Israel's dispersion.[18] While the "Hebrew approach" works for Jeremiah, it seems very unlikely in the case of Sol 9:2. The subject matter of Sol 9 suggests that the reference to Deut 28:25 was worked into the text in a stage of Greek composition. The simplest explanation of such a phenomenon is to submit that the Psalm was created from the start in Greek.

## 3.6. Identifying the proof text

An additional difficulty with the "Hebrew approach" needs to be pointed out here. If the Psalms of Solomon were created in Hebrew, its allusions would have contained elements of a Hebrew source text. In order to convey the allusion, the translator who created the Greek text of the Psalms of Solomon would have needed to recognize which passage was referred to. This would have been hard for some of the passages in which the Hebrew text and the Septuagint diverge, and particularly so with some of the more laconic allusions:

**Sol 8:9**
υἱὸς μετὰ μητρὸς καὶ πατὴρ μετὰ θυγατρὸς **συνεφύροντο**
they committed incest, son with mother and father with daughter

Ezek 22:6
ἕκαστος πρὸς τοὺς συγγενεῖς αὐτοῦ **συνανεφύροντο** ἐν σοί
each with his kindred, they wallowed together in you.
אִישׁ לִזְרֹעוֹ הָיוּ בָךְ

18 It is to be noted that the Psalm alludes to the Deuteronomy passage very loosely. Although the thought is the same, practically the only word that is common to the two passages is precisely the word διασπορά. This means that if Sol 9 had been written in Hebrew, it would have been very hard for the translator to identify the scriptural passage referred to. See below in section 3.6.

everyone according to his power has been bent on shedding blood

The variant reading of the Septuagint in Ezek 22:6: "each toward his family members" (for MT's "each according to his might," see above) triggered the interpretation of "they were" (הָיוּ) as a reference to incestuous intercourse. This understanding was then expressed through the verb συνανεφύροντο (or συνεφύροντο), "they mixed together." In Sol 8:9, it is this verb that references the passage in Ezekiel. A case like this raises the question how a putative translator of the Psalms of Solomon's Hebrew original would have been able to identify the allusion to the proof text. Even if the interpretation we know from the Septuagint was applied by readers to the Hebrew text of Ezekiel, there would be no obvious clear reference point in the Hebrew text of Sol 8:9 to which the allusion could be attached.

Similarly, in 9:2, the allusion to Deut 28:25 hinges on the word διασπορά, "diaspora." Recognizing Deut 28:25 as the intertext would have been a challenge in Hebrew.

In a final example, a textual variant combines with an interpretational divergence, thus potentially making it even harder to match the proof text to its Greek translation:

**Sol 15:3**
**ἐν ὀργάνῳ ἡρμοσμένῳ**
with the tuned instrument

2 Sam/2 Kgds 6:5
**ἐν ὀργάνοις ἡρμοσμένοις**
with tuned instruments

בְּכֹל עֲצֵי בְרוֹשִׁים
on all manner of instruments made of fir wood

The parallel to 2 Sam 6:5, 1 Chron 13:8, reads here: בְּכָל־עֹז וּבְשִׁירִים "with all might, and with songs," and 4QSam[a] has this same reading in the Samuel text. This still doesn't bring us to the Greek reading, although it brings us closer. The Greek rendering of 2 Kgds 6:5 is plausibly retroverted as בכלי עז "with instruments of praise," a text that is otherwise unattested.[19] None of these Hebrew phrases would be of much help in recognizing the allusion.

19 See Eugene Ulrich, *The Biblical Qumran Scrolls*, VTS 134 (Leiden: Brill, 2010), 298.

If we suppose the Psalms of Solomon were composed in Greek, this problem disappears. In each of these examples, the allusion is indexed by a striking (and rare) Greek expression which conforms precisely to the Greek text alluded to.

## 3.7. Conclusions

Close study of the scriptural allusions in Psalms of Solomon indicates that the Septuagint features we find there are native. The available data converge to show that the features go back to the original first century BCE composition, which was written in Greek. This makes the Psalms of Solomon a very early witness to the text of the Septuagint. Admittedly, the style of the allusions generally does not allow the precision necessary to use the readings in textual criticism of the Septuagint. In Psalm 119/118:28 the text used by the author of Sol 16 must have read ἐνύσταξεν "slumbered," not ἐστέναξεν as in one minuscule, nor ἔσταξεν as in Rahlfs' edition (conjectured on the basis of the MT). In Ezek 22:6, the allusion confirms the reading συνεφύροντο of Pap. 967 against συνανεφύροντο as in the Alexandrinus. But otherwise, the scriptural allusions contribute very little to the textual criticism of the passages referred to. The significance of the Psalms of Solomon for the textual history of the Septuagint lies elsewhere.

In regard to the Psalms of Solomon themselves, the most important conclusion this chapter leads to is that they are a Greek composition. Several scholars have recently advocated this view, with good arguments.[20] The Hebrew-like character of the Greek text is not necessarily a sign of translation Greek, for purported Hebraisms may in fact be "Septuagintisms." Moreover, some of the grammar and vocabulary of the Psalms of Solomon is untypical of Greek texts translated from Hebrew, and parts of the text are hard to render into a Semitic language (see further in section 5.1).

Other writings from the same period present a profile similar to that of the Psalms of Solomon. The Book of Judith, long held to be a translation from Hebrew, has in recent times come to be regarded as a Greek composition. Judith is written in Septuagintal language and exhibits many features typical of translation Greek. Its scriptural

20 See Albrecht, *Psalmi Salomonis*, 181–182.

references are all from the Septuagint, however, and some linguistic features speak strongly in favor of a Greek origin.[21] The Prayer of Azariah incorporated into the Septuagint version of Daniel 3 is another example. Its style is Septuagintal throughout, partly because much of it is made up of allusions and semi-quotations from the Greek version. Many scholars hold it to be a translation from Hebrew. But no Hebrew version of the prayer, nor of any part of it, has survived. A good case can be made for original composition in Greek.[22] Taken together, these writings illustrate a trend to create books in the style of the Septuagint—a phenomenon attested to a lesser extent in Wisdom of Solomon and continuing in later writings such as the gospel of Luke or Joseph and Aseneth.

While Judith and Greek Daniel likely reflect a background in Egypt, the Psalms of Solomon were composed in first-century BCE Jerusalem. This makes the writing unique: as far as we know, no other religious literature originating in Jerusalem was written in Greek in this period. But its uniqueness does not make it unthinkable. Greek was widely spoken in Jerusalem and Judah by the second half of the first century BCE. Moreover, as was hinted at above, the Psalms of Solomon reveal through many details that the community among which they came into being had strong connections to the diaspora. That Jews from the diaspora should have settled in Jerusalem and continued to speak Greek there, including in their meetings as a religious group is eminently plausible.[23] Naturally, they would continue using the Septuagint version as scripture. Just such a group could well have formed the milieu that produced the Psalms of Solomon.[24]

---

21 See e.g. Jeremy Corley, "Septuagintalisms, Semitic Interference, and the Original Language of the Book of Judith," in *Studies in the Greek Bible: essays in honor of Francis T. Gignac, S.J*, ed. Jeremy Corley, Vincent Skemp (Washington DC: Catholic Biblical Association, 2008), 65–96.

22 See Jan Joosten, "The Prayer of Azariah (DanLXX 3): Sources and Origin," in *Septuagint and Reception*, ed; J. Cook, VTS 127 (Leiden: Brill, 2009), 5–16.

23 The Theodotus synagogue inscription, probably to be dated to the first century CE, illustrates both the presence of Greek-speaking religious groups in Jerusalem and their ties to the diaspora. For the date of the inscription, see John S. Kloppenborg, "Dating Theodotos (CIJ II 1404)," *Journal of Jewish Studies* 51 (2000), 243–280.

24 See now Anneli Aejmelaeus, "The Origins of the *Kaige* Revision," in *Scriptures in the Making: Texts and Their Transmission in Late Second Temple Judaism*, ed. Raimo Hakola, Paavo Huotari, Jessi Orpana, CBET 109 (Leuven: Peeters, 2022), 285–311.

# 4.
# Psalms of Solomon's Text of Scripture: A Revised Septuagint

As was argued in the preceding chapter, the scriptural allusions in the Psalms of Solomon as we have them reflect the work of the authors. The Psalms are a Greek composition, whose intertextual references interact with Greek texts. In most cases, the textual basis of the allusions conforms to the Septuagint. This indicates that the authors, who were active in Jerusalem during the latter part of the first century BCE, read their scriptures in this Greek version.

In eight passages, however, the allusions diverge from the Septuagint in a way that suggests a different textual basis. In some cases the allusion appears to presuppose a text that stands closer to the MT than to the Septuagint, in other cases its vocabulary is not that of the Old Greek but of a later version. Some allusions follow the Septuagint in part but diverge from it in a crucial detail.

Allusions that diverge from the Septuagint text may raise the question whether there is an allusion at all. The absence of verbal agreements with an attested Greek text leaves only the content from which to divine the intertextual nature. Perhaps, therefore, one or two cases should be rejected. Even in this case, however, enough examples of non-Septuagintal features remain for our puzzlement. How should such features be explained?

The explanation needs to be sought within the parameters defined in chapter 3. Although non-Septuagintal features in the allusions align in part with the Hebrew text, they do not suffice to overturn the conclusions reached so far. The original language of the Psalms of Solomon is Greek, and the allusions to scripture were for the most part formulated in reference to the Septuagint version. Within this framework, several approaches seem possible. The divergences, or some of them, may simply reflect the freedom of the authors.

Alternatively, the authors, in addition to using the Septuagint may have referred to other forms of scripture. Perhaps they were bilingual and took account of the Hebrew text as well as the Septuagint? A third possibility is that the mixture was present in their text of scripture; the authors of the Psalms of Solomon may have been using a revised text of the Septuagint.

In the present chapter, the divergent allusions will be analyzed with a view to determining their background. I will argue that the third explanation is on the whole the most likely. The text of scripture underlying the Psalms of Solomon was a partially revised Septuagint. This conclusion will be bolstered with a number of additional arguments. Some features other than allusions have a bearing on the issue.

## 4.1. Scriptural allusions diverging from the Septuagint

> Sol 5:3
> οὐ γὰρ λήψεταί τις σκῦλα παρὰ ἀνδρὸς δυνατοῦ
> For no one will take booty from a strong man.
>
> Isa 49:24
> μὴ λήμψεταί τις παρὰ γίγαντος σκῦλα;
> Shall one take booty from a giant?

While elements of the Septuagint of Isa 49:24 can be recognized in the allusion, there are divergences too. In part these may be attributed to the author's freedom. The change from a rhetorical question to a statement reflects the different rhetorical frameworks: in Isaiah, what looks impossible at first sight—the people's return from captivity—turns out to be about to happen, and is therefore justly presented as a question. In Sol 5, the parable illustrates something that is really unthinkable: that humans should take something against God's will. The more classical form of the verb in Sol 5 is not sufficiently certain to make anything of.[1] The different word order may be a free variation.

1 Many verbal forms in the Psalms of Solomon are suspect of being later corrections, as argued originally by Oscar von Gebhardt, *ΨΑΛΜΟΙ ΣΟΛΟΜΩΝΤΟΣ: Die Psalmen Salomo's zum ersten Male mit Benutzung der Athoshandschriften und des Codex Casanatensis* (Leipzig: Hinrichs, 1895), 30–34.

One wonders, however, about the difference between "giant" and "strong man." This might be another free alteration. But the fact that Sol 5's reading corresponds to the Hebrew suggests otherwise:

הֲיֻקַּח מִגִּבּוֹר מַלְקוֹחַ

Shall booty be taken from a *strong man*?

The Septuagint's "giant" is an interpretive rendering perhaps indebted to Aramaic.[2] In biblical Hebrew, גבור properly means "hero, mighty man." Note that Symmachus corrects to δυνατός in this verse, and the same correction is found for Aquila and Thedotion in other passages.[3] The alignment of the allusion with this less fanciful interpretation likely reflects the biblical text the author was using.

As said, the allusion is not entirely independent from the Septuagint. Part of the vocabulary goes with the Greek version of Isa 49:24, and so does the grammatical construction. While the MT has the verb in the passive, both the Septuagint of Isa 49:24 and Sol 5:3 have the active.[4] The scriptural allusion would appear to stand somewhere between the Hebrew and the Greek. The mixture may be due to the author's having an eye on the two texts at once: he borrowed part of the allusion from the Septuagint, but realizing that "giant" wasn't in accord with the Hebrew text he corrected it to "strong man." Another possibility is that the textual basis of the allusion was a corrected Septuagint. The reading of Symmachus illustrates that revisions of the Septuagint exhibit this type of correction. Symmachus' version is too late to envisage any type of connection with the Psalms of Solomon, but revisions of the Septuagint were already in circulation in the first century BCE.

**Sol 7:3**
σὺ ἐν θελήματί σου παίδευσον ἡμᾶς
Discipline us by your will

2 See Randall Buth et al., "γίγας," in *Historical and Theological Lexicon of the Septuagint*, ed. Eberhard Bons (Tübingen: Mohr Siebeck, 2020), 1853–1864, in part. 1856–1857.

3 See e.g. Aquila in Gen 6:4. Note that in the NT, the allusion to the same passage employs a different adjective, ἰσχυρός: Mark 3:27; Matt 12:29; Luke 11:21-22.

4 The addition of indefinite τίς in the two texts would seem to confirm the connection, but in Sol 5:3 τίς is not attested in the manuscripts. See note 24 in chapter 1.

Hos 10:10
ἦλθεν παιδεῦσαι αὐτούς,
he has come to educate them.

If Sol 7:3 alludes to Hos 10:10, as argued in chapter 1, its scriptural basis cannot be the Old Greek. The Septuagint translator read the first word of Hos 10:10 as a form of the verb בוא "to come."[5] The basis of the allusion is not the Septuagint, but stands closer to the received Hebrew text:

בְּאַוָּתִי וְאֶסֳּרֵם
It is in my desire that I should chastise them (KJV)

Whether the source of the allusion should be the Hebrew text itself or a Greek version is impossible to say on the basis of the available data.[6]

**Sol 9:9**
σὺ **ᾑρετίσω** τὸ σπέρμα Αβρααμ παρὰ πάντα τὰ ἔθνη
You chose the offspring of Abraham above all the nations.

Isa 41:8
Σὺ δέ, Ισραηλ, παῖς μου Ιακωβ, ὃν **ἐξελεξάμην**, σπέρμα Αβρααμ, ὃν ἠγάπησα
But you, Israel, my servant, Iakob, whom I have chosen, the offspring of Abraam, whom I have loved.

Although a connection between these two passages is fairly certain, the verb expressing the idea of election is not the same. Instead of ἐκλέγομαι the allusion has the synonym αἱρετίζω for Hebrew בחר "to choose, to elect." To account for the change one might first of all point to Sol 17:4, which speaks of the election of David. In the Septuagint, this motif is always expressed with the verb ἐκλέγομαι,[7] but the author of Sol 17:4 uses αἱρετίζω instead. Thus, the change in Sol 9:9 may reflect the author's predilection for this verb in the meaning "to elect."[8]

5 The reading ἦλθεν is that of all the manuscripts, but Ziegler in the Göttingen edition adopts the conjecture ἦλθον "I came."

6 Unfortunately, no minor Greek versions are attested for this verse, though perhaps the Vulgate preserves an echo of Symmachus or Aquila: *iuxta desiderium meum corripiam eos* "according to my desire I will chastise them." Note, however, that the Vulgate appears to reflect a Hebrew variant, כאותי "according to my desire," while the allusion in Sol 7:3 reflects the MT's באותי "in my desire."

7 See e.g. 2 Chron 6:6; Psal 78/77:70.

8 Note that ἐκλογή in Sol 9:4; 18:5 does not refer to election but to free choice.

It is also possible, however, that the allusion reflects a Greek version other than the Septuagint. No data are available for Isa 41:8, but in Judg 5:8, the use of αἱρετίζω for בחר is reported for Theodotion.

**Sol 11:7**
Ἔνδυσαι, Ιερουσαλημ, τὰ ἱμάτια τῆς δόξης σου
Put on, O Ierousalem, the garments of your glory

Isa 52:1
ἔνδυσαι τὴν ἰσχύν σου, Σιων, καὶ ἔνδυσαι τὴν δόξαν σου, Ιερουσαλημ
Put on your strength, O Sion, and put on your glory, O Ierousalem

The difference between "put on your glory" in the Septuagint of Isa 52:1 and "put on the garments of your glory" in Sol 11:7 may seem trifling. The notion of clothing is implicit in the verb "to put on." Nevertheless it deserves to be noted that the allusion conforms on this point to the Hebrew:

לִבְשִׁי עֻזֵּךְ צִיּוֹן לִבְשִׁי בִּגְדֵי תִפְאַרְתֵּךְ יְרוּשָׁלַםִ
Put on your strength, O Zion, put on your glorious garments, O Jerusalem

Thus the divergence could reflect the author's text of scripture. If so, he was either casting a sideways glance at the Hebrew, or he used a revised Septuagint. Note that Theodotion and Symmachus have τὰ ἱμάτια τῆς δόξης σου in Isa 52:1, exactly as we read in Sol 11:7.

As was noted in chapter 1, the parallel between Sol 11 and Bar 4–5 includes the reference to Isa 52:1. The allusion in Bar 5:1 does not have τὰ ἱμάτια "the garments," however, and seems to reflect the Old Greek of Isa 52:1. Fuller discussion of the parallel will be offered in the Appendix.

**Sol 16:2**
παρ᾽ ὀλίγον ἐξεχύθη ἡ ψυχή μου εἰς θάνατον
But for a little my soul was poured out to death

Isa 53:12
ἀνθ᾽ ὧν παρεδόθη εἰς θάνατον ἡ ψυχὴ αὐτοῦ
because his soul was given over to death

תַּחַת אֲשֶׁר הֶעֱרָה לַמָּוֶת נַפְשׁוֹ
because he poured out himself (lit. "his soul") to death

While the Septuagint has the multi-purpose verb "to deliver," the allusion in Sol 16:2 uses a more picturesque expression: "to pour out" (the soul).

The notion of "pouring out one's (or someone else's) soul" is found a few times in the Hebrew Bible.[9] This makes it possible to argue that the author used a biblical expression without having a specific verse in mind.

However, "to pour out" is one of the meanings expressed by the verb used in the Hebrew text of Isa 52:12, ערה *hiphil* "to empty, to pour out." No minor versions are attested for Isa 52:12, but the equivalence between ערה "to pour out" and a composite of Greek χέω is attested in Lam 4:21 (וְתִתְעָרִי—καὶ ἀποχεεῖς). The "Septuagint" version of Lamentations is a representative of the *kaige*-Theodotion group.[10] Thus the variation in Sol 16:2 from the Septuagintal text could be due to an early revision of the Greek text of Isaiah.

> **Sol 17:1**
> ἐν σοί, ὁ θεός, καυχήσεται ἡ ψυχὴ ἡμῶν
> In you, O God, shall our soul boast
>
> Psalm 34/33:3
> ἐν τῷ κυρίῳ ἐπαινεσθήσεται ἡ ψυχή μου
> In the Lord my soul shall commend itself
>
> בַּיהוָה תִּתְהַלֵּל נַפְשִׁי
>
> My soul makes its boast in the Lord

If there is an allusion, as was argued in chapter 1, it does not appear to reflect the text of the Septuagint. There is no good reason to think the author modified the Septuagint version because he had an eye on the Hebrew text. The form תִּתְהַלֵּל is correctly translated by either verb, the one used in Psalm 34/33:3 or the one used in Sol 17:1. The lexical change may be a free alteration on the part of the author, but it is equally possible that the author was referring to a non-Septuagintal Greek version. Aquila corrected ἐπαινεσθήσεται to καυχήσεται "shall boast" in this verse, and this correction may well go back to earlier revisions of the *kaige*-Theodotion type.

---

9 "Pouring out one's soul": 1 Sam 1:15; Psalm 42:5; Job 30:16; Lam 2:12 (LXX ἐκχέω in all four passages); "pouring out someone else's soul": Psalm 141:8 (LXX differently).

10 See Kevin, J. Youngblood, "Lamentations," in *The T&T Clark Companion to the Septuagint*, 500–519.

**Sol 17:3**
ἡμεῖς δὲ ἐλπιοῦμεν ἐπὶ τὸν θεὸν σωτῆρα ἡμῶν
But we will hope in God our savior

Mic 7:7
Εγὼ δὲ [...] ὑπομενῶ ἐπὶ τῷ θεῷ τῷ σωτῆρί μου
But as for me [...] I will wait for God my savior
וַאֲנִי [...] אוֹחִילָה לֵאלֹהֵי יִשְׁעִי
But as for me [...] I will wait for the God of my salvation

If it is correct to find an allusion to Mic 7:7 in Sol 17:3, the reference does not seem to be to the Septuagint. As in the preceding passage, interference from the Hebrew text of Micah seems unlikely: since both ὑπομένω and ἐλπίζω render the Hebrew well, knowledge of the Hebrew text would hardly incite the author to change the one to the other. Instead, the author may have made the change on his own account. In the Psalms of Solomon, ὑπομένω is used three times, always in the sense "to endure (discipline, etc.)."[11] Since this meaning did not fit the present context, the author may have decided to change it to ἐλπίζω "to hope," which is frequent in the Psalms of Solomon.

It remains possible, however, that the allusion is based on a non-Septuagintal version. Although none of the minor versions is attested for this passage in Mic 7:7, the equivalence between Hebrew יחל and ἐλπίζειν is attested for Theodotion and Aquila elsewhere.[12]

**Sol 17:23–24**
ἐκτρῖψαι ὑπερηφανίαν ἁμαρτωλοῦ ὡς σκεύη κεραμέως,
ἐν ῥάβδῳ σιδηρᾷ συντρῖψαι πᾶσαν ὑπόστασιν αὐτῶν
to smash the arrogance of the sinner like a potter's vessel,
to shatter all their substance with an iron rod.

Psalm 2:9
ποιμανεῖς αὐτοὺς ἐν ῥάβδῳ σιδηρᾷ,
ὡς σκεῦος κεραμέως συντρίψεις αὐτούς.
You shall shepherd them with an iron rod,
and like a potter's vessel you will shatter them.

The reference to Psalm 2:9 is certain, but instead of pairing "to shepherd" with "to shatter" as in the Septuagint, Sol 17:23–24 repeats the notion of breaking. This agrees with the MT:

11 See 10:2; 14:1; 16:15.
12 Thus for Theodotion in Job 14:14; Isa 42:4; Mic 5:6; for Aquila in Job 14:14; Isa 42:4 (all rendering the piel).

תְּרֹעֵם בְּשֵׁבֶט בַּרְזֶל כִּכְלִי יוֹצֵר תְּנַפְּצֵם

You shall break them with a rod of iron
you shall dash them in pieces like a potter's vessel

The divergence can hardly be attributed to free rewriting, it must reflect some type of contact with the Hebrew. More specifically, since the difference between "to break" and "to shepherd" depends solely on the vocalization (*təroʿēm* "you will shatter" versus *tirʿēm* "you will shepherd"), the text of the allusion reflects knowledge of the reading tradition later encoded in the Masoretic vowels. The author of Sol 17 may have known of the traditional reading of Psalm 2, and may have decided to adjust the Septuagintal text he was alluding to accordingly. Alternatively, he may have used a revised Septuagint in which ποιμανεῖς "you will shepherd" had been corrected so as to align with the received Hebrew. A reading meaning "you will break"—retroverted from the Syriac as συντρίψεις or συνθλάσεις—is reported for Symmachus.

Looking back on the eight cases, two categories can be recognized. While in all cases the divergence agrees with the Hebrew text, some involve differences of interpretation (5:3; 7:3; 11:7; 16:2; 17:23–24), while others merely show the replacement of one word by a near synonym (9:9; 17:1; 17:3). The explanation from free rewriting applies more easily to the latter instances. Because the authors of the Psalms of Solomon are known to modify their intertexts, they may well in some cases have adapted the vocabulary, even at the risk of obscuring the reference. In two examples, moreover, a possible reason for the change was suggest (αἱρετίζω in 9:9; ἐλπίζω in 17:3). The explanation of free rewriting is less likely for the cases of divergent interpretation, because it requires attributing the correspondence with the Hebrew to accident.

Conversely, the explanation from dual use of Septuagint and Hebrew scriptures in producing the allusions would account for the cases involving different interpretations, but it is less effective in explaining the change of synonyms: why would a glance at the Hebrew lead the author to change the wording?

The third explanation proposed above, attributing the divergences to the Greek text of scripture the authors were using could account for all the cases. In seven out of eight cases the non-Septuagintal feature of the allusion is attested in one or other minor version, either in the verse in question or in other passages with the same Hebrew lexeme. The only exception is the allusion to Hos 10:10 in Sol 7:3.

The discussion up to this point can be summed up in a table: in five cases, the divergence between the Septuagint reading and the reading reflected in the Psalms of Solomon is due to interpretation, in three cases it reflects the use of a synonym; in four instances, the non-Septuagint reading is attested for minor versions in the verse itself, in two it is attested for the same Hebrew term in a different verse (in one instance, 7, 3, it is not attested at all):

| Sol | interpretation | synonym | attested in verse | attested elsewhere |
|---|---|---|---|---|
| 5:3 | x | | x | |
| 7:3 | x | | | |
| 9:9 | | x | | x |
| 11:7 | x | | x | |
| 16:2 | x | | | (x)[13] |
| 17:1 | | x | x | |
| 17:3 | | x | | x |
| 17:23f | x | | x | |

The frequent alignment of the allusions, where they diverge from the Septuagint, with the minor versions is hardly due to chance. Aquila, Symmachus and Theodotion are usually situated in the second century CE, which makes them too late to have influenced the Psalms of Solomon. However, Barthélemy, and others before and after him, have demonstrated that the minor versions did not fall from the clear sky, but stood in a long tradition of revising the Septuagint text so as to make it agree more closely with the emerging Masoretic text.[14] Aquila and Theodotion very often go hand in hand, but Symmachus too, in spite of its different translation technique, belongs to the same family.

While the beginning of revisional activity on the Septuagint is hard to trace, many scholars agree that by the second half of the first century BCE it had been underway for some time. The Greek Twelve-Prophets scroll from Nahal Hever, whose text represents a rather systematic revision of the Septuagint according to the principles of Theodotion,

13 With variation between ἐκχέω in Sol and ἀποχέω in Lam 4:21.

14 See Dominique Barthélemy, *Les devanciers d'Aquila : première publication intégrale du texte des fragments du dodécaprophéton trouvés dans le désert de Juda, précédée d'une étude sur les traductions et recensions grecques de la Bible réalisées au premier siècle de notre ère sous l'influence du rabbinat palestinien* (Leiden: Brill, 1963). For the impact and evaluation of Barthélemy's study, see Robert Kraft, "Reassessing the Impact of Barthélemy's *Devanciers* Forty Years Later," *BIOSCS* 37 (2004), 1–28.

has been dated to that period on paleographic grounds.[15] What all this means is that revised texts of the Septuagint could have been available to the authors of the Psalms of Solomon. It is therefore legitimate to use the minor versions as evidence of earlier attempts to bring the Septuagint into line with the Hebrew.

There is no reason of principle to explain all our cases in the same way. Lack of evidence may mean the alleged allusion to Hos 10:10 in Sol 7:3 needs to be dealt with separately. And perhaps one or two of the synonymous variants are to be attributed to chance. Even so, the way the data line up suggests that the impact of a revised text of the Septuagint was a factor in the production of scriptural allusions in the Psalms of Solomon. In the next two sections, I will present two additional types of evidence confirming this hypothesis.

## 4.2. Scriptural phrases

As chapter 2 illustrates, the influence of scripture on the Psalms of Solomon far exceeds the category of allusions. Terminology, idiomatic expressions, and features of syntax and style are borrowed from the Greek version all through the corpus. Many of these borrowings throw little light on the question of the text consulted by the authors. When they agree with the Septuagint, they confirm the use of that version, but when they diverge it is usually impossible to determine whether they reflect a revised Septuagint, other sources, or simply the free writing of the author.

An exception is to be made for set phrases that recur in scripture. Where such a phrase turns up in the Psalms of Solomon, it cannot be regarded as an allusion to a specific passage, but it does go back to the text of scripture. If it takes on a specific form that differs from the Septuagint, the use of a modified Greek version may be suspected. If in addition the wording in the Psalms of Solomon agrees with a later recension, this suspicion hardens into a viable hypothesis.

---

15 See notably Peter J. Parsons in E. Tov, with the collaboration of R. A. Kraft and a contribution by P. J. Parsons, *The Greek Minor Prophets Scroll from Nahal Hever (8HevXIIgr)*, The Seiyal Collection 1, DJD 8 (Oxford: Clarendon Press, 1990), 19–38.

## "Forever and again"

Five times in the Psalms of Solomon one encounters the formula εἰς τὸν αἰῶνα καὶ ἔτι "forever and again" (Sol 9:11; 11:7, 9; 17:1, 46). The phrase recalls the liturgical formula לְעוֹלָם וָעֶד "forever and ever" attested in Exod 15:18, Mic 4:5 ; Dan 12:3 and six times in the Psalms (9:6; 45:18; 119:44; 145:1, 2, 21); a variant form without the initial preposition is attested six times too, all of them again in Psalms (10:16; 21:5; 45:7; 48:15; 52:10; 104:5). Strikingly, none of these occurrences is rendered in the Septuagint with the exact wording of the Psalms of Solomon. In Psalms, the two variants are mostly translated as εἰς τὸν αἰῶνα καὶ εἰς τὸν αἰῶνα τοῦ αἰῶνος (sometimes in abbreviated form). The adverb ἔτι occurs in Exod 15:18 (τὸν αἰῶνα καὶ ἐπ' αἰῶνα καὶ ἔτι), but otherwise the formula differs from the version we find in the Psalms of Solomon.

In the minor versions too, ἔτι turns up as an equivalent of עד. Notably, the Theodotionic text of Dan 12:3 has εἰς τοὺς αἰῶνας καὶ ἔτι, and Aquila has εἰς αἰῶνα καὶ ἔτι in Ps 21/20:5; 45/44:7 for עוֹלָם וָעֶד. Both of these are close to the wording in Psalms of Solomon, though not identical.

One text, however, almost certainly coincided exactly with the wording we are looking for. It is well known that the Twelve-Prophets scroll from Nahal Hever (8HevXII) contains a revision of the Septuagint text in the spirit of Theodotion, and that Justin Martyr's quotations from the Minor Prophets overlap with this ancient text. In Mic 4:5, the Septuagint reads εἰς τὸν αἰῶνα καὶ ἐπέκεινα "forever and beyond." 8HevXII is damaged here and only two relevant letters ([...εἰς τ]ὸν [αἰῶνα...]) can be read. Justin quotes the passage in *Dialogue with Trypho* 109. The sole extant manuscript reads, in the relevant passage: εἰς τὸν αἰῶνα καὶ ἔσται, which appears to be corrupt. Recent editors of the *Dialogue* agree to emend this to εἰς τὸν αἰῶνα καὶ ἔτι.[16] Barthélemy reconstructs the same form for the text of the scroll.[17]

16 See Miroslav Marcovich, *Iustini Martyris Dialogus cum Tryphone* (Berlin & New York NY, De Gruyter, 1997).

17 Barthélemy, *Devanciers*, 206. Tov (*Greek Minor Prophets Scroll*, 39, 87) leaves a blank in his reconstruction and suggests either ἔτι or ἐπέκεινα as possible readings in the lacuna. The lacuna is situated at the bottom of column, thus not allowing us to reason from the available space.

The reconstructed reading of the *kaige* revision of Mic 4:5 coincides precisely with the version quoted in the Psalms of Solomon. The rendering of Aquila is to be viewed as a further refinement of the reconstructed *kaige* rendering.

## "For victory"

As was pointed out in chapter 2, the Psalms of Solomon have titles reminiscent of the titles of biblical Psalms. The heading of Sol 8 reads as follows: Τῷ Σαλωμων· εἰς νῖκος "Pertaining to Solomon, to victory." The specification "to victory" does not seem to be a reference to the contents of the Psalm. Instead, the phrase εἰς νῖκος is most likely a refraction of the formula למנצח "for the director of music" (?), which in the Septuagint is generally rendered as εἰς τὸ τέλος "to the end."[18]

In biblical Hebrew, the meaning of the root נצח most often has to do with everlastingness, a meaning which may have led to the Septuagint rendering. In Ezra and Chronicles the verb נצח is used a few times in the sense "to oversee," from which the most common interpretation of למנצח in the Psalms titles, "for the director of music," is derived. But in later Hebrew and Aramaic the verb means "to defeat, to be victorious." This meaning underlies the renderings of למנצח in the minor versions. Aquila regularly translates the phrase as τῷ νικοποιῷ "to the one causing victory" and Symmachus as ἐπινίκιος "(song) of victory." In Theodotion, למנצח is most often translated εἰς τὸ νῖκος, but in Psalm 13/12:1 the equivalent is εἰς νῖκος, exactly as we have it in Sol 8:1.[19] The agreement between Sol 8:1 and the rendering recorded for Theodotion in Psalm 13/12:1 is almost certainly not a matter of happenstance. It attests knowledge on the part of the author of Sol 8 of revisional efforts of the type that have left a trace in the version of Theodotion used by Origen in his hexapla.

A complication to this explanation arises in Sol 1. The title of Sol 1 is insecurely transmitted in the manuscripts. Several editors do not reconstruct a title at all.[20] The Göttingen edition, however, does give a title: Ψαλμὸς τῷ Σαλωμων· εἰς τέλος "Psalm of Solomon, to the end."

18 Rahlfs edits the conjecture νεῖκος "(for) strife."
19 Ryle & James, *Psalms of the Pharisees*, 74.
20 Thus notably Rahlfs' edition. For discussion, see Gebhardt, *Psalmen Salomo's*, 47.

This reconstruction goes back to a conjecture of Perles, who takes εἰς τέλος from the end of the first line of Sol 1 and moves it up to the title. The logic of this operation is that εἰς τέλος, as a reflex of למנצח fits the title well, whereas its meaning in the first verse is unclear. If the reconstructed text were correct, it would mean that two different equivalents of למנצח figure in the titles of the Psalms of Solomon. As it seems, however, the reconstruction of the title of Sol 1 is excessively speculative. It is true that εἰς τέλος sits somewhat oddly in Sol 1:1a:

Εβόησα πρὸς κύριον ἐν τῷ θλίβεσθαί με εἰς τέλος,
I cried to the Lord when I was completely distressed

However, many other passages in the Psalms of Solomon are slightly bizarre, for whatever reason. We should leave εἰς τέλος where it is.[21] This means the term למנצח, typical as it is of the titles of Psalms, finds only one echo in the Psalms of Solomon, an echo which does not follow the formulation of the Septuagint but agrees with a rare rendering in Theodotion.

## 4.3. Vocabulary

The key characteristic of the revisions of the Septuagint, particularly of Aquila and Theodotion, is their translation technique.[22] They follow the received Hebrew more closely than the Old Greek. This aspect of the revisions provides little purchase on their possible proximity to the Psalms of Solomon. However, the drive for closer alignment with the source text also entails innovations in the realm of vocabulary. The revisers use words that are not found in the Septuagint, or use them in a new way. Some of these innovations turn up in our corpus too, thus again suggesting some type of exchange or community between the authors of the Psalms of Solomon and the *kaige*-Theodotion/proto-Aquila tradition.

---

21 Cf. Sol 2:5; 17:35 (εἰς αἰῶνα).

22 In the search of points of contact between the Psalms of Solomon and the *kaige*-Theodotion group, some features attested only for Aquila have been included on the understanding that Aquila is a continuation of the process begun in these texts.

### i) ἀποικεσία "exile"

**Sol 9:1**
Ἐν τῷ ἀπαχθῆναι Ισραηλ ἐν ἀποικεσίᾳ εἰς γῆν ἀλλοτρίαν
When Israel was led away in exile in a foreign land

The ἀποικ- word-group generally refers to exile in the Septuagint and writings that stand in its shadow.[23] Within this group, the verb ἀποικίζω and the nouns ἀποικία and ἀποικισμός are well attested in classical Greek literature. But ἀποικεσία is almost wholly limited to the Septuagint and writings dependent on it. Even so, the word is very rare. Apart from Sol 9:1, ἀποικεσία occurs in 2 Kgs/4 Kgds 19:25; 24:15; 25:27, and four times in 2 Esdras (Ezra 6:16, 19, 20, 21). Both these writings belong to the *kaige* group. The passages in 4 Kgds are found in the γδ section identified by Thackeray, whose revisional character was demonstrated by Barthélemy. It is to be noted that instead of ἀποικεσία, the Antiochene text reads ἀποικισμός in 2 Kgs/4 Kgds 24:15. This may indicate that the Old Greek of Reigns used the latter noun, and that ἀποικεσία is a revisional feature.[24] As to 2 Esdras, its close ties with the *kaige*-Theodotion group are well known.[25] To my knowledge, the word is not attested for Theodotion or Aquila.

Although Sol 9:1 does not allude to a precise passage in scripture, it is hard to avoid the conclusion that its use of ἀποικεσία indicates some form of familiarity with revisions standing in the *kaige*-Theodotion tradition.

### ii) καταφορά "deep sleep"

**Sol 16:1**
Εν τῷ νυστάξαι ψυχήν μου ἀπὸ κυρίου παρὰ μικρὸν ὠλίσθησα
ἐν καταφορᾷ ὑπνούντων μακρὰν ἀπὸ θεοῦ

23 Outside of these texts, the word-group mostly refers to voluntary displacements. See Stefanie Peintner (Plangger), Georg Fischer, "ἀποικία κτλ," in *Historical and Theological Lexicon of the Septuagint*, ed. Eberhard Bons (Tübingen: Mohr Siebeck, 2020), 937-954.

24 As Barthélemy has demonstrated, in the *kaige* sections of 2–4 Kingdoms, the Antiochene text has at times preserved the unrevised Old Greek. In the γδ section, however, it appears to have preserved relatively little of the Old Greek.

25 See e.g. Timothy Janz, *Deuxième livre d'Esdras*, La Bible d'Alexandrie XI 2 (Paris: Cerf, 2010), 151–164.

> When my soul slumbered, away from the Lord, I slipped for a short time,
> in the lethargy of those that sleep far from God.

In the meaning "lethargic attack," the noun καταφορά is attested in Greek literature from Hippocrates onward, mostly in medical texts. The word is not found in the Septuagint. In Aquila it is attested several times as the equivalent for Hebrew תרדמה "deep sleep."[26] Although Sol 16:1 does not seem to allude to a definite passage, the motif of deep sleep as a figure of estrangement from God has biblical models.[27] The use of the rare word καταφορά in Sol 16:1 and Aquila is hardly due to accident, and most likely reflects an exegetical tradition known to both circles.

### iii) συνταγή "assignation, appointment"

> **Sol 4:5**
> ἐν ὀφθαλμοῖς αὐτοῦ λαλεῖ πάσῃ γυναικὶ ἐν συνταγῇ κακίας
> With his eyes he speaks with every woman in an evil get-together

The noun συνταγή is rare in Greek literature. As a verbal noun derived from συντάσσω it naturally expresses meanings such as "order, command," and "physician's prescription." It occurs twice in the Septuagint, in Jud A 20:38 (B σημεῖον) and Ezra 10:14. Both times it refers to an agreed or appointed meeting, a meaning connected to the middle of the verb, συντάσσομαι "to agree." Ezra 10:14 belongs to the *kaige* group, as was indicated above, and it is therefore no surprise to find συνταγή again in the minor versions. It is attested for Aquila as a rendering of Hebrew מועד "meeting, place or time of meeting" in Num 3:7; 4:25; 1 Sam 9:24; 13:8; 20:35; Ps 74:4; 75:3; Isa 33:20, and, for the same equivalent, it is found in Symmachus in Num 3:7; 4:25; 1 Sam 13:8,[28] and in Theodotion in 1 Sam 20:35.

In addition, Aquila uses συνταγή several times in Ezekiel to render Hebrew זמה "wicked plan": Ezek 16:58; 22:9; 23:27, 29, 44, 48. The rendering probably reflects a type of biliteral analysis whereby the root זמם was identified with the root זמן "to appoint."[29] Contextually, most

26 Gen 2:21; 1 Sam 26:12; Prov 19:15; Isa 29:10.
27 See Isa 29:10; Jonah 1:5, 6; Ps 12/11:4.
28 Note also Prov 1:26.
29 For συνταγή as a translation of a word formed from the root זמן, see Ezra 10:14.

of the occurrences in Ezekiel depict situations of sexual impropriety, thus inviting the meaning "assignation, rendezvous." This is precisely the meaning συνταγή appears to express in Sol 4:5. As in the previous example, the usage of a rare word in the Psalms of Solomon and Aquila suggests an interpretative tradition underlying both writings.

Perhaps other words could be listed to argue for proximity between the Psalms of Solomon and the *kaige*-Theodotion-Aquila group. The use of the words ὑποκρίνω and ὑπόκρισις in reference to religious hypocrisy, as discussed briefly in chapter 2, are found in Sol 4 and in the minor versions.[30] They are absent from the main corpus of the Septuagint. However, the verb does occur several times in the Greek version of Ben Sira, with the specific meaning of "pretending to be righteous while sinning in secret." Since this version is older than the earliest witnesses to the *kaige*-Theodotion group, it is hard to argue for a link specifically between the Psalms of Solomon and the recensions of the Septuagint. As it seems, the use of this word group in inner-Jewish polemics predates the Psalms of Solomon by two generations or so.

In one passage we find ἀνωφελής "useless" in reference to sin:

> **Sol 16:8**
> And let not the beauty of a woman who transgresses the law deceive me,
> Nor of anything that is subject to useless sin (ἁμαρτίας ἀνωφελοῦς).

In the minor versions, this adjective is a standard equivalent of און "iniquity."[31] Neither the meaning in Sol 16, nor the reason for the usage in the minor versions is perfectly clear, however. This makes it hard to know whether there is a connection. In the Septuagint, the adjective is found a couple of times in reference to idolatry.[32]

## 4.4. Conclusions

A small number of scriptural allusions in the Psalms of Solomon diverge from the wording of the Septuagint while adhering in one way or another to the received Hebrew. As I have tried to demonstrate, this

30 See notably the Theodotionic additions to Job 34:30; 36:13.
31 As noted by Ryle & James, *Psalms of the Pharisees*, 122–123.
32 See Isa 44:10; Jer 2:8.

is almost certainly not due to accident, and probably reflects at least in part the impact of recensional processes aligning the Old Greek with the emerging Masoretic text. Building on the results of the previous chapter we may formulate the following hypothesis. The Psalms of Solomon were composed in Greek in reference to a Greek version of the scriptures the authors cherished. The Greek version in question was the Septuagint, but not the pure Old Greek. Instead, it was a Septuagint adjusted here and there to the Hebrew text according to the principles known from the *kaige*-Theodotion-Aquila tradition.

This is an exciting conclusion, but it is not a highly surprising one. If one had asked a knowledgeable Septuagint scholar what a sample of Septuagint text as read and studied in Jerusalem during the first century BCE might have looked like, she or he would probably have allowed for an Old Greek basis partly contaminated with *kaige*-like readings. Our conclusion ties in with, and thus confirms, several widely-shared postulates of Septuagint studies. Notably, the data indicate that something like the *kaige* revision was already being carried out around the middle of the first century BCE, and that this revision was located in the homeland.

The hypothesis does not imply that the authors of the Psalms of Solomon used the *kaige* recension as such. Alongside the eight places where the allusion aligns with the MT stand many places where the allusion aligns with the Septuagint, against the MT (see chapter 3).[33] The text of scripture underlying the Psalms of Solomon may have been a Septuagint text that was superficially affected by a number of readings taken from an early recension. Alternatively, it may reflect an early stage in the revision, when the adjustment with the Hebrew had not yet been carried out systematically.

It would be a mistake to conclude that the authors of the Psalms of Solomon are to be identified with the initiators of the *kaige* revision. Well-known markers of that revision, such as the use of the composite particle καί γε, are never found in the Psalms of Solomon. Moreover, no reviser of the Septuagint would have alluded as often as the authors of the Psalms of Solomon did to the Septuagint where it diverges markedly from the received Hebrew. The two groups were distinct.

33 Note also that the allusion to Dan 12:2 in Sol 3:12 aligns more with the Septuagint than with Theodotion.

Nevertheless, there are some similarities: both circles are heavily invested in the Jewish scriptures, and both write in Greek. Their date and place are close. The Psalms of Solomon were composed in Jerusalem in the aftermath of Pompey's conquest of the city in 63 BCE. The *kaige* recension is first attested in 8HevXII, a manuscript found in a cave near the Dead Sea and penned most probably during the second half of the first century BCE. In all likelihood the *kaige* revision was produced in or near Jerusalem (see further in chapter 5).

# 5.
# Historical Implications

Our analysis of the textual profile of scriptural allusions in the Psalms of Solomon has exposed the two-sided nature of the corpus. While some aspects point to the western diaspora, other aspects reveal a close connection to the homeland. The fact that the allusions consistently reflect the Septuagint suggests a link with the Judaism of Egypt, where the Greek translation of scripture originated and had taken a central place in Jewish life. Although they were living in Jerusalem at the time of Pompey's conquest, the authors of the Psalms of Solomon, or their ancestors, would appear to have migrated there from abroad and kept strong ties with Jews of the dispersion. Alongside the Septuagint, however, we see a minor textual strand going back to an early revision. The tendency to revise the Old Greek so as to bring it closer to the emerging standard of the proto-Masoretic text is in all likelihood to be localized in Judea. If the Septuagint represents the diasporic heritage of the authors, the traces of revision epitomize what happened to them in Jerusalem.

In the present chapter we will draw some conclusions and point out perspectives for future study. We will look first at the diasporic heritage of the Psalms of Solomon, then at the way they interact with new developments in the homeland.

## 5.1. The original language of the Psalms of Solomon

Most scholars consider the Psalms of Solomon to have been composed in Hebrew.[1] This judgment reflects, firstly, the general likelihood that a religious work of this type, written in Judea in the first

1 Alternatively, they could be composed in Aramaic, although for the Psalms of Solomon this hypothesis is not seriously defended by anyone. For the role of Aramaic in Judean Judaism of the Second Temple period,

century BCE, would have been composed in Hebrew.[2] While many new Jewish texts were composed in Greek in this general period, as far as we know practically all of them originated in the western diaspora.[3] Secondly, the scholarly judgment is based on a number of hard passages, which philologists have tried to illuminate through reverse engineering. When the Greek is translated back into the original Hebrew, the thought becomes clear—at least, so it is claimed. A good example is the following:

> **Sol 2:25**
> Do not delay, O God, to repay them on their heads,
> to declare in dishonor the arrogance of the dragon
> (τοῦ εἰπεῖν τὴν ὑπερηφανίαν τοῦ δράκοντος ἐν ἀτιμίᾳ)

"The dragon" is a figure of Pompey, but the second stich is puzzling. What does it mean to "declare" something in dishonor? Wellhausen proposed a characteristically brilliant solution: if τοῦ εἰπεῖν reflects Hebrew לאמר, "to say,"[4] perhaps the Hebrew translator erred and the genuine text was להמיר, "to change" (or the late form למיר with elision of the *he*):

> Do not delay, O God, to repay them on their heads,
> to change into dishonor the arrogance of the dragon

---

see, for instance, *Aramaica Qumranica. Proceedings of the Conference on the Aramaic Texts from Qumran in Aix-en-Provence 30 June–2 July 2008*, ed. Katell Berthelot, Daniel Stökl Ben Ezra (Leiden: Brill, 2010).

2 See most recently Martha Himmelfarb, "The Pseudepigrapha in Greek: Translation, Composition, and the Diaspora," in *The Old Testament Pseudepigrapha: Fifty Years of the Pseudepigrapha Section of the SBL* (EJL 50, SBL 2019), 263–286, in particular 278–279.

3 This is almost certainly true of the original Greek compositions that ended up in the Septuagint canon, see Jan Joosten, "The Origin of the Septuagint Canon," in *Die Septuaginta - Orte und Intentionen,* ed. Siegfried Kreuzer, Martin Meiser, Marcus Sigismund, WUNT 361 (Tübingen: Mohr Siebeck, 2016), 688-699. It is true too for other Jewish literature in Greek from this period. For an overview of the relevant works, see Emil Schürer, *The History of the Jewish People in the Age of Jesus Christ (175 B.C.-A.D. 135),* English Version Revised and Edited by Geza Vermes, Fergus Millar, Martin Goodman (Edinburgh: T&T Clark, 1986), 470–594.

4 A possible problem with this hypothesis is that (τοῦ) εἰπεῖν is not a frequent equivalent of Hebrew לאמר (although it is attested, see Jer 37/30:1).

The thought would be reminiscent of Hos 4:7: "I will change their glory into shame."

Wellhausen proposed several other possible cases, and other scholars added more.[5] If any of these conjectures were correct, the case for Hebrew as the original language would be proven. But the procedure is problematic, and its results remain fragile. Several other possible explanations have been proposed for Sol 2:25b, some of them supposing a different mistranslation from Hebrew and some supposing a corruption within the Greek tradition. Moreover, many other passages in the corpus present difficulties of interpretation that cannot be solved by retroversion into Hebrew.

It is said that hard cases make bad law. Instead of building on difficult passages, I have argued in chapter 3 that we should look to passages whose import is clear, and whose implication is that the text must have been created in Greek. In a number of places, the logic of the Psalms of Solomon exploits distinct readings in the Septuagint. There is no easy way to account for this phenomenon on the supposition that the text was created in Hebrew.

Other arguments have been developed in favor of a Hebrew origin. The Greek Psalms of Solomon exhibit a large number of Hebraisms. But almost all of them can with equal right be considered Septuagintisms. They do not require the songs to be translated from Hebrew. An author composing in Greek in close dependence on Septuagintal style could be expected to produce this type of language. Finally, several scholars have argued that the Syriac version of the Psalms of Solomon reflects independent knowledge of the Hebrew source text.[6] However, much evidence shows that the Syriac depends on the Greek text without any input from a Hebrew source.[7]

---

5 Notably Felix Perles.

6 See e.g. Joseph L. Trafton, *The Syriac Version of the Psalms of Solomon: A Critical Evaluation*, SCS 11 (Atlanta: Scholars Press, 1985). This line of argument appears to have gone out of fashion in recent times.

7 With regard to the topic of the present work, it is interesting to note that several scriptural allusions are given in the Syriac version in wording that makes it nearly impossible to recognize the intertext, whether in Hebrew, Greek or Syriac. See for instance Sol 3:4, where hardly anything in the Syriac reminds one of Prov 3:11; see also Sol 3:9 (Lev 5:18); Sol 11:3 (Num 31:6); Sol 15:3 (2 Sam 6:5).

An additional argument in favor of a Greek origin is that the songs are hard to translate into Hebrew.[8] Some of the Greek syntax does not correspond to Hebrew patterns. A phrase like "the hope and the refuge of the poor" (ἐλπὶς καὶ καταφυγὴ τῶν πτωχῶν, 15:1) would in ancient Hebrew be formulated: "the hope of the poor and their refuge," as the syntax of the construct state requires.[9] In the translated books of the Septuagint, only the Hebrew pattern is regularly attested. Some of the vocabulary too has no ready equivalent in Hebrew: ποικιλία ἁμαρτιῶν, "a variety of sins" (4:3), works well in Greek, but it is difficult to put into Hebrew. In the translated books, ποικιλία does occur, but mostly with its original meaning of "embroidery."[10] Similar examples are found throughout the corpus. Notably, a number of philosophical terms seem to be completely alien to the Hebrew of the time.[11]

As a modest confirmation of the Greekness of our corpus, it is interesting to note what happens in some of the scriptural allusions. In chapter 2 we observed how the authors of the Psalms of Solomon

---

8 The Hebrew translation of Frankenberg is full of infelicities, see Wilhelm Frankenberg, *Die Datierung der Psalmen Salomo's. Ein Beitrag zur jüdischen Geschichte*, BZAW 1 (Giessen: J. Ricker, 1896), 63–85. The unpublished translation of Delitzsch is an improvement, but still has many problematic expressions. The translations of Kamenetzky and Stein conform to Hebrew diction, but often stray from the meaning of the Greek text, see Abraham S. Kamenetzky, "*Tehillot Shelomoh*," *Hashiloah* 13 (1904), 43–55.149–159 and Menahem Stein, "*Mizmorey Shelomoh*," in *Hasepharim Hahitsonim*, ed. A. Kahana (Tel Aviv: Meqorot, 1936/37), 431–462. For an overview of Hebrew translations of the Psalms of Solomon, see Harald Samuel, "Albert Renovanz: „*Tehillim shelli-Shelomo* – Die Psalmen Salomo's ins Hebräische übersetzt"," *leqach* 9 (2009), 79–117.

9 See Jan Joosten, "Reflections on the Original Language of the Psalms of Solomon," in *The Psalms of Solomon: Language, History, Theology*, ed. E. Bons, P. Pouchelle, Early Judaism and Its Literature 40 (Atlanta: SBL, 2015), 31-47, in particular 39.

10 See e.g. Exod 27:16; Judg 5:30. In Sir 43:26 the word is used for Hebrew מין, the "variety" of living creatures.

11 See Eberhard Bons, "Philosophical Vocabulary in the Psalms of Solomon: The Case of Ps. Sol. 9:4," in *Psalms of Solomon* (above, note 8), 49–58; Eberhard Bons, "Psalms of Solomon 16:10 and Its Biblical and Hellenistic Backgrounds," in *The Psalms of Solomon: Texts, Contexts, and Intertexts*, ed. G. Antony Keddie, Patrick Pouchelle, Kenneth Atkinson, EJL 54 (Atlanta: SBL, 2021), 23–33.

modify extracts from scripture so as to adapt them to their rhetorical strategies. Strikingly, this transformation at times goes hand in hand with an adaptation to Greek diction:

- Sol 1:3 ἐν τῷ […] με […] πολλὴν γενέσθαι ἐν τέκνοις "when I […] had become rich in children"
  The expression πολλὴ ἐν τέκνοις, "rich in children," reflects the Hebrew phrase רַבַּת בָּנִים, literally: "numerous of children," in the text alluded to (1 Kgds 2:5). In Hebrew, such a phrase cannot be split, the syntax of the construct state requires the two words to figure in sequence. In applying this expression to Jerusalem, in her soliloquy, the author of Psalms of Solomon broke it up in a way that is impossible to reproduce in Hebrew.
- Sol. 3:2 ὅτι ἀγαθὸς ψαλμὸς τῷ θεῷ ἐξ ἀγαθῆς καρδίας "for a psalm to God from a good heart is good"
  The addition "from a good heart" to the words quoted from Psalm 147/146:1 is congenial to the pious approach characterizing the Psalms of Solomon. But the diction is not Hebraic. In the Hebrew Bible, the "good heart" always refers to joy and satisfaction, generally in the context of meals.[12] This is not what is meant in Sol 3:2, where the phrase refers to the right attitude of the worshiper. The expression "good heart" as a metaphor for sincerity and devotion is distinctively Septuagintal.[13]
- Sol 3:4 οὐκ ὀλιγωρήσει δίκαιος παιδευόμενος ὑπὸ κυρίου "The righteous does not despise being disciplined by the Lord"
  Instead of "not despising *discipline*," as in Prov 3:11, Sol 3 has the righteous "not despising *being disciplined*." The transformation produces an elegant expression in Greek, which is hard to render into Hebrew. The Hebrew participle is not used with the "circumstantial" function instantiated in Sol 3:4. Note also that with passive verbs the agent usually remains unnamed in ancient Hebrew.[14]

12 See Judg 16:25; 2 Sam 13:28; 25:36; 1 Kgs 8:66; 2 Chron 7:10; Prov 15:15; Esth 1:10; 5:9; Eccl 5:7.

13 See Prov 14:33 (MT לֵב נָבוֹן "an understanding heart"); 1Chr 29:19 (MT לֵבָב שָׁלֵם "a perfect heart"); Judith 8:28 Πάντα, ὅσα εἶπας, ἐν ἀγαθῇ καρδίᾳ ἐλάλησας (non-translated).

14 The use of ὑπό "by" to designate the agent is found a few times in the Septuagint (e.g. Exod 5:14; 16:3; Deut 33:29), but it is relatively far more common in Psalms of Solomon (Sol 3:4; 4:19; 6:2, 2; 8:34; 11:2; 15:9; 16:15; 17:26).

- Sol 4:3 ἡ χεὶρ αὐτοῦ ἐν πρώτοις ἐπ᾽ αὐτὸν ὡς ἐν ζήλει "And his hand is the first upon him as if in zeal"
  In a phrase tagged on to the words borrowed from Deut 17:7, comparative ὡς is used with the connotation of "under the pretence of."[15] This usage is found also in Sol 4:5 "he is quick to enter every house cheerfully ὡς ἄκακος as though innocent."[16] It is not attested elsewhere in the Septuagint.[17] While ὡς is the standard equivalent of Hebrew *k*- "as" in the Septuagint, the present usage is not attested with the Hebrew preposition, nor is there an easy way to translate ἐν ζήλει in this verse into Biblical Hebrew.
- Sol 4:20 ὀφθαλμοὺς ἐκκόψαισαν κόρακες ὑποκρινομένων "may ravens peck out the eyes of hypocrites"
  While in Prov 30:17 those who disrespect their parents are the target of the curse, Sol 4:20 takes aim at the hypocrites. The change occasioned an elegant hyperbaton in Greek, which can in no way be reproduced in Hebrew. In Hebrew the only possible position for "hypocrites" is after "eyes."
- Sol 15:3 ἐν ὀργάνῳ ἡρμοσμένῳ γλώσσης "with the tuned instrument of the tongue"
  While evoking the "tuned instruments" that David used when bringing up the ark of the Lord (2 Sam/2 Rgs 6:5, 14), the author of Sol 15 modified the phrase so as to define the human voice as the prime means of praising God. By adding the genitive γλώσσης, he created a nominal phrase impossible to reproduce in Hebrew—again, because of the syntax of the construct state. Hebrew would require the genitive to be positioned immediately after the substantive noun, not after the adjective.

Where we see the Greek text diverging from its scriptural model, we also note the use of Greek features that do not have an equivalent in ancient Hebrew. The creativity of the authors expresses itself in Greek.

It is hard to overturn a consensus that has lasted for centuries. Nevertheless, the time has come seriously to consider the possibility

15 See William Arndt and F. Wilbur Gingrich, *A Greek-English Lexicon of the New Testament*, Second Edition (Chicago: University of Chicago, 1979), s.v. ὡς III.3 "(ὡς) introduces a quality wrongly claimed."

16 See also Sol 8:11, 30.

17 Muraoka, *Lexicon*, ὡς 12, p. 749.

that the Psalms of Solomon were not translated from Hebrew but created from the start in Greek.

## 5.2. The milieu of the Psalms of Solomon

The conclusion with regard to the original language raises the question how we can account for the use of Greek in a religious writing created in Jerusalem during the first century BCE. As was indicated above, we know of no other examples of Jewish works from this time and place written in Greek. Rather than leading into a dead end, however, this question directs our attention to an important aspect of the corpus, namely the connection to the Jewish diaspora.[18] Among Jews of the western diaspora, Greek would have been the main means of communication and religious expression. Scripture would be read in Greek, without reference to a Hebrew source text. A connection to the diaspora would explain the use of Greek in the Psalms of Solomon. As it seems, although the authors lived in Jerusalem, they had strong ties with the diaspora and may themselves have originated there.

Exile and the dispersion of the Jews are important themes in the Psalms of Solomon.[19] Some of the references, it is true, are merely traditional: Israel has been taken into exile for its sins (9:2-3), but God will bring them back in his mercy (8:28); their return will be an event full of grace and wonder (11:2-6; 17:26, 31, 44). But other passages betray a more original view of the diaspora. Reminiscing about a period before the present crisis, Jerusalem, personified as a mother, evokes her former prosperity:

> **Sol 1:3-4**
> I thought in my heart that I was full of righteousness,
> when I prospered and had become rich in children.
> Their wealth was spread over the whole earth,
> and their glory to the end of the earth.

Jerusalem's children are not only the ones living in the city. If their wealth and glory, which is really Jerusalem's own, is spread out over the

18 See the interesting study of Julia Rath, "Exile and Diaspora in the Psalms of Solomon," in *The Psalms of Solomon: Collected Essays*, ed. Felix Albrecht, Kenneth Atkinson, Patrick Pouchelle, Parabiblica 1 (Tübingen: Mohr Siebeck, 2023), 49–68.

19 See 1:4; 8:23, 28; 9:2–3; 11:2–6; 17:16–18, 26-28, 44.

entire earth it is because the children are too. In other words, Jerusalem is envisaged here as the metropolis of many settlements, a world-wide network of prosperous satellites.[20] The exile is not seen as a disaster but as a success story. Admittedly, in the narrative of Sol 1 this view turned out to be false. But that was not because the idea of exile was essentially flawed, but because Jerusalem's children "became insolent in their prosperity" and sinned.

A possible allusion to scripture may be relevant at this point, although its figurative language makes it hard to interpret:

> **Sol 8:23**
> God was justified in his judgments among the nations of the earth,
> and the devout of God are *like lambs* innocent in their midst.

This is possibly an allusion to Mic 5:7:

> And *the remnant of Jacob among the nations*, in the midst of many peoples,
> shall be like dew falling from the Lord and *like lambs* in the grass

There is hardly any lexical overlap between these passages—for which reason it was not included among the cases gathered in chapter 1—but the surprising image is partly the same.[21] If the thought is that Israelites are a lamb-like presence among the nations, this would imply a very positive view of the diaspora. Alternatively, however, these verses may state that the Israelites are present as one nation among many.

In one passage, the relations between the diaspora and the group that produced the Psalms of Solomon seems to be mentioned explicitly:

> **Sol 17:16-18**
> Those who loved the congregations of the devout fled from them,
> as sparrows were scattered from their nest.
> They wandered in wildernesses that their souls be saved from evil,

---

20 Cf. Isaac L. Seeligmann, "Yerushalaim be-Mahshevet ha-Yehadut ha-Hellenistit," in idem, *Studies in Biblical Literature*, ed. Avi Hurvitz, Sara Japhet, Emanuel Tov (Jerusalem: Magnes, 1996), 396–410 [Hebrew].

21 The image is also specific to the Septuagint, the MT of Mic 5:7 speaks of "showers of rain" (in parallel with "dew").

> and their saved soul was precious in the eyes of those who sojourned abroad (παροικία).
> They were scattered over the whole earth by lawless men

Having been forced to leave Jerusalem, members of the group that produced the Psalms of Solomon were taken in by "those who sojourned abroad"—Jews of the dispersion.[22]

In aggregate, the references to exile leave little doubt that this is a theme close to the authors' heart. They speak about their co-religionaries abroad with warmth and appreciation. One will not go wrong in supposing that the discourse on the diaspora is rooted in personal acquaintance. All this speaks for the view that the group that produced the songs consisted of diaspora Jews, or descendants of diaspora Jews, who lived in Jerusalem while keeping in close contact with similar-minded groups abroad. This filiation alone accounts for the use of Greek and the Greek version of scripture. Greek was widely spoken in Jerusalem by the mid-first century BCE and it had made inroads in various parts of public and private life. But in the religious sphere it had by no means replaced Hebrew and Aramaic. Also, the central position of the Hebrew scriptures remained uncontested in the homeland.[23]

## 5.3. The "diasporic worldview"

The suggestion of a connection to the diaspora is further strengthened when we pay attention to peculiar features of the piety and worldview expressed in the corpus.

It is a striking fact that although the Jerusalem temple plays an important part in the Psalms of Solomon, it is never presented as the dwelling-place of God. Instead, God, or God's name, dwells with his people.

> **Sol 7:1**
> Remove not your dwelling from us, O God,
> lest they attack us, those who hated us without cause.[24]

---

22 For παροικία as a term designating the diaspora, see Ryle and James, *Psalms of the Pharisees*,135–136.

23 Possibly with the help of an Aramaic Targum.

24 See also Sol 7:6 (which alludes to Ezek 43:7, see chapter 1): "While your name dwells in our midst, we shall find pity, and no nation will prevail against us."

> **Sol 9:9**
> You chose the offspring of Abraham above all the nations,
> and you placed your name upon us, O Lord[25]

The community of the pious is the dwelling place of God's name.[26]

The temple is important as a symbol, but it plays no role in the daily life of the devout. The sanctuary, the altar, and the sacrifices are mentioned several times, always to deplore that they were polluted by wicked Israelites or gentiles.[27] The authors never mention that they participated in the temple cult in the past, nor do they express the hope to do so again in the future. Their personal religious practice is situated elsewhere.

As we saw in chapter 3, instead of seeking forgiveness by means of temple sacrifice, the Psalms of Solomon underscore the importance of personal piety:[28]

> **Sol 3:8**
> he made atonement for sins of ignorance by fasting and humiliation of his soul

Other functions of sacrifice, too, are replaced with cultic acts that are not dependent on the temple.

> **Sol 15:3**
> the fruit of the lips with the tuned instrument of the tongue
> the *first fruit* of the lips (ἀπαρχὴν χειλέων)[29] from a devout and righteous heart

First fruits, ἀπαρχή, are a type of sacrifice (see e.g. Exod 22:8; Lev 22:12; Num 5:9) brought to the temple according to the law. In Sol 15:3 they

---

25 See Sharon, *Judea under Roman Domination*, 319.

26 Noah Hacham, "Where Does the Shekhinah Dwell? Between Dead Sea Sect, Diaspora Judaism and Rabbinic Literature," in *The Dead Sea Scrolls in Context: Integrating the Dead Sea Scrolls in the Study of Ancient Texts, Languages, and Cultures*, vol. 1, ed. A. Lange, E. Tov, M. Weigold, (Brill: Leiden, 2011), 399–412.

27 See 1:8; 2:2, 3; 8:11, 12

28 See Büchler, *Types of Jewish-Palestinian Piety*, 170–195. Büchler points out that the authors of the Psalms of Solomon differ markedly on this point from early figures of the Pharisaic-Rabbinic movement as described in later Midrashic literature.

29 Instead of χειλέων, the Göttingen edition adopts the conjecture χειρῶν "hands," with good arguments. For the point at issue, this textual variation makes no difference.

are spiritualized. The stance does not seem to be polemical, it is rather a question of personal experience. While the authors and the readers recognize the temple and its cult as sacred institutions, their own piety is exercised elsewhere.

Nadav Sharon has perceptively connected this set of ideas with what he calls a "diasporic worldview."[30] God is not tied to a place, but to a community. Away from the temple, the notion gained relevance that personal behavior can in some cases stand in for sacrificial worship.

## 5.4. The "diasporic worldview" and the Septuagint

In chapter 2, we saw how the authors of the Psalms of Solomon develop relatively novel ideas by grafting them onto passages from scripture. In retrospect it is easy to see that this process in several cases exploits the Greek version of scripture specifically. As Greek speakers, reading the scriptures in Greek, the authors were steeped not only in Septuagint phraseology but also in the thought-world projected in the version. The Septuagint is, for the most part, a translation of Hebrew writings, but that does not mean it has no distinctive features. Without falling into a facile "Hebrew thought" versus "Greek thought" dichotomy, it is legitimate to recognize that certain terms and concepts were imported into the Septuagint from its Hellenistic *Umwelt*.[31]

The concept of divine education is central to the Psalms of Solomon, and the words παιδεύω, "to educate," παιδεία, "education," παιδευτής, "educator," provide the means to develop it in a coherent manner (see chapter 2). In this respect, the Psalms of Solomon go beyond the Hebrew scriptures, where the discourse on divine education is not yet expressed by means of specialized vocabulary. But παιδεύω and its congeners come to prominence already in the translated books of the Septuagint. They are the standard equivalents of derivates of the Hebrew root יסר, "to correct, to discipline," and they are used also for other equivalents such as בין, "to understand" (Deut 32:10; see also Dan

30 Sharon, *Judea under Roman Domination,* 317–319.

31 See the interesting reflections of Christoph Kugelmeier, "Bibel, Papyri und Philosophen: Beobachtungen zur Geschichte hellenistischer Abstraktbegriffe," in *Septuagint Vocabulary. Pre-History, Usage, Reception,* ed. Eberhard Bons, Jan Joosten (Atlanta : SBL, 2011), 25–44.

1:20), or שבט, "rod" (Job 37:13). Moreover, in several passages this vocabulary seems to occur as a *Verlegenheitsübersetzung*, when the translator is unable to make sense of the Hebrew: thus the difficult נשקו בר, "kiss the son (?)," in Ps 2:10 is rendered "accept education" (δράξασθε παιδείας), and the morally dubious "a bribe is like a magic stone in the eyes of those who give it" in Prov 17:8, becomes "education is a gracious wage to them that use it."[32] It is fair to say, then, that the terminological innovation in the Psalms of Solomon, and the ensuing unification of the theme of divine education, were prepared in the Septuagint of the translated books.

To a lesser extent this is true too for the motif of hypocrisy. As in the case of παιδεύω and its derivatives, the word ὑποκριτής and its congeners occur in the Septuagint before they do so in the Psalms of Solomon.[33] We may also note that the Hebrew of Psalm 53 had nothing to say on this theme, but the Greek translator of Psalm 52 found occasion to insert the figure of the "man-pleasers," which adumbrates the importance of the motif of hypocrisy in later writings. The allusion to Psalm 53/52:6 in Sol 4:19 is not only a stepping-stone for the author, but also a theological paradigm: the wicked *par excellence* are the deceivers, who pretend to observe God's law but transgress it in secret.

The conception of Jerusalem as a center for Jews worldwide, noted above in section 6.2, also develops hints in the Septuagint. Jerusalem is referred to as a "metropolis" in the Greek version of Isa 1:26, and as "Mother Sion" in Ps 86/87:5, both times deviating from the Hebrew source text.[34] A little later, this view of Jerusalem is developed by Philo (*Flaccus* 45–46; *Legat.* 281).[35]

Jews in the western diaspora show a growing readiness to describe Jewish teaching and experience in terms borrowed from Greek. This is a complex process. It is difficult to tell to what extent different languages correspond to different realities. Also, it is important not to draw the distinction between Judaism in Egypt and Judaism in Jerusalem too

32 See also Psalm 18/17:36; 90/89:10; Prov 19:18; Am 3:7. See the extensive discussion of such passages in Pouchelle, *Dieu Éducateur*, 278–320.

33 See notably Sir 32:15; 33:2.

34 See Seeligmann, "Yerushalaim."

35 Sarah Pearce, "Jerusalem as 'Mother-City' in the Writings of Philo of Alexandria," in *Negotiating Diaspora: Jewish Strategies in the Roman Empire*, ed. John M. G. Barclay (T&T Clark, 2004), 19–37.

starkly—in the Hellenistic period, all Jews were Hellenized to some extent.[36] Nonetheless, we can recognize a trajectory, which runs from the translated books in the Septuagint through the non-translated books and reaches a high point in Philo—arguably it continues in the Church Fathers. Along this trajectory, biblical motifs are interpreted by the help of Greek concepts. The Psalms of Solomon stand halfway along this trajectory.[37]

An interesting theme in this regard is that of moderation. The need for moderation is a prominent idea in the Hebrew scriptures, expressed in such central passages as the manna-story (Exod 16), the law of the King (Deut 17), or Amos' social criticism. Nevertheless, there does not seem to be a word meaning "moderation" in biblical Hebrew.[38]

In Greek culture, moderation is central too. It is "the greatest virtue" according to Heraclitus.[39] The overarching term is σωφροσύνη, "temperance, moderation, prudence, purity, decorum, self-control."[40] Many other Greek words express the notion of the "golden mean," sufficiency without excess.

In the Psalms of Solomon, the idea of moderation occupies an important position.[41] God directs the chosen people and forgives the

36 See e.g. Martin Hengel, *Judentum und Hellenismus: Studien zu ihrer Begegnung unter besonderer Berücksichtigung Palästinas bis zur Mitte des 2 Jh.s v. Chr.* (Tübingen: Mohr, , 1969); ET by John Bowden: *Judaism and Hellenism: Studies in Their Encounter in Palestine during the Early Hellenistic Period* (London: SCM Press; Philadelphia: Fortress, 1974).

37 A beautiful illustration of this process is explored in Bons, "Psalms of Solomon 16:10."

38 Similarly, Biblical Hebrew does not have a word for "immoderation, excess," corresponding to Greek ἀκρασία, which is attested in Sol 4:3. Note, however, ἀκρατής "unrestrained" in Prov 27:20a, without Hebrew counterpart.

39 Heraclitus DK112 (http://heraclitusfragments.com/index.html).

40 The word is not attested in the translated books of the Septuagint. It does make an appearance in some of the non-translated books: in an addition to Esther, 2 & 4 Maccabees and Wisdom of Solomon. Its presence in Sol 10:8 is uncertain: it is read in several manuscripts, probably with the support of the Syriac version, but other manuscripts read εὐφροσύνη. Rahlfs adopts the latter reading, Albrecht the former.

41 For an analysis of the socio-economic background of the Psalms of Solomon, see G. Anthony Keddie, "Poverty and Exploitation in the Psalms of Solomon: At the Intersection of Sapiential and Apocalyptic Discourses,"

sins of the devout. But he also provides for their bodily needs. Excess leads to arrogance, which typifies the wicked.[42] Therefore God will give the right amount:

> **Sol 16:12**
> Support my soul with goodwill and cheerfulness;
> when you strengthen my soul, *what is given will be sufficient for me.*

In chapter 2 we saw how Isa 49:24—the vignette of the strong man from whom one cannot take booty—is forced into a straitjacket so as to support the notion of divine providence in Sol 5:3. We also saw how in Sol 17:33 an allusion to the law of the king (Deut 17:17) pictured the coming Messiah as a moderate person himself. What is presently of interest is that the author expresses the notion by means of Greek terms that are relatively new in Jewish writing:

> **Sol 5:10**
> Μακάριος οὗ μνημονεύει ὁ θεὸς ἐν συμμετρίᾳ αὐταρκείας·
> ἐὰν ὑπερπλεονάσῃ ὁ ἄνθρωπος, ἐξαμαρτάνει.
> Happy is the man whom God remembers in due proportion to sufficiency;
> if man has too much, he sins.

In the meaning "symmetry, due proportion, harmony," συμμετρία defines one of the characteristics of beauty and goodness in Greek writing. It has no ready equivalent in ancient Hebrew, and the noun is not found in the Septuagint. The adjective occurs once, in Jer 22:14, "you built yourself a well-proportioned house (οἶκον σύμμετρον)."

The noun αὐτάρκεια, "self-sufficiency," is also absent from the Septuagint, but the adjective αὐτάρκης and the verb αὐταρκέω do occur. In fact, αὐτάρκης is found in a passage that may have inspired the authors of Sol 5:

> Prov 30:8b-9
> give me neither riches nor poverty, but order what is necessary and sufficient for me (σύνταξον δέ μοι τὰ δέοντα καὶ τὰ αὐτάρκη) lest I be filled and become a liar and say: "Who sees

in *The Psalms of Solomon: Texts, Contexts, and Intertexts*, ed. G. Antony Keddie, Patrick Pouchelle, Kenneth Atkinson, EJL 54 (Atlanta: SBL, 2021), 81–110.

42 See 1:6; 2:1, 2, 26, 27; 17:6.

> me?" Or lest I become poor and steal and swear by the name of God.

Although there is no phraseological overlap, the connection between self-sufficiency and the danger of excess occurs in both passages. The adjective is found in the sense "self-sufficient" also in Sir 40:18 "The life of a self-reliant and a hard-working person will be sweet." The verb is found in the Pentateuch:

> Deut 32:10
> He made him self-sufficient in a desert land (αὐτάρκησεν αὐτὸν ἐν γῇ ἐρήμῳ), in thirst of heat, in a waterless place.

The precise meaning of the verb in this context is debated. Brenton translates "he maintained him," and Muraoka proposes the gloss "to supply with necessities."[43] As against this, both the *Bible d'Alexandrie* ("rendre quelqu'un auto-suffisant") and NETS underscore the etymological meaning. More important than the precise meaning is the interpretation the verb expresses. According to the Hebrew text, the Lord *found* (מצא) Israel in the desert. The interpretive rendering of the Septuagint, which agrees with that of Targum Onqelos, harks back to the Pentateuchal stories about how God provided for his people during their wanderings in the desert.[44] The most archetypal of these stories is the one on the manna (Exod 16): God miraculously sustained his people with daily bread. The translator of Exodus did not find occasion to use a word of the αὐταρκ- group, but the story beautifully encapsulates the idea.

In Philo's interpretation of the manna story we encounter both the the αὐταρκ- group and the notion of due proportion:[45]

> *Alleg.* 3:163
> "Let the people indeed go forth and the whole system of the soul likewise, and let it collect science and begin knowledge, not in large quantities but from day to day." For, in the first place, in that way it will not exhaust all at once the abundant

43 Lancelot C. L. Brenton, *The Septuagint with Apocrypha: Greek and English* (London: Bagster: 1851).

44 See notably Num 11:22.

45 See Peter Tomson, *'Voor één dag genoeg': het brood, het Woord en de wetenschap* (Brussels: Universitaire Faculteit voor Protestantse Godgeleerdheid, 1993), in particular 11–18.

> riches of the grace of God: but it will overflow like a torrent with their superfluity. Secondly, it will happen that when they have taken such good things as are sufficient (αὐτάρκη) for them and duly measured (μεμετρημένα), they will think God the dispenser of the rest.

We should be wary of over-interpreting these data. There is no reason to think the author of Sol 5 had the manna-story in mind, nor that Philo knew the Psalms of Solomon. Nevertheless, the various passages quoted illustrate an itinerary. They show, firstly, that the Septuagint translators here and there tried out Greek terms that had no ready equivalent in Hebrew in order to express ideas they found in the source text and, secondly, that the authors of the Psalms of Solomon—like Philo and other readers of the Septuagint—took note of some of these terms and elaborated upon them.

The point of this section is not that Greek-speaking Jews betrayed their religious identity and exchanged Hebrew concepts for Greek ones. The adoption of the Greek terms discussed goes hand in hand with a transformation of their content: "education," "hypocrisy" and "moderation" started out as Greek notions without ready equivalent in biblical Hebrew, but by the time of they turn up in the Psalms of Solomon they have been thoroughly integrated into a new worldview.[46] Nevertheless, the adoption of Greek concepts is significant on the Jewish side too. Scriptural notions are distilled and enriched by the help of Greek philosophical terms. The Psalms of Solomon represent a modest step along this trajectory.

46 As was mentioned in chapter 2, Zurawski has recently argued that the notion of education we find in the Psalms of Solomon owes almost nothing to the Greek ideal of *paideia*, see Jason Zurawski, "Solomonic Paideia: Divine Pedagogy in the Psalms of Solomon and the Book of Wisdom," in *The Psalms of Solomon: Collected Essays*, ed. Felix Albrecht, Kenneth Atkinson, Patrick Pouchelle, Parabiblica 1 (Tübingen: Mohr Siebeck, 2023), 85–100. Although this is going too far, in my view, he is correct in pointing out the great differences that exist between the usage in our corpus and in Greek writings that are not Jewish in origin.

## 5.5. Traces of a revised Septuagint

Alongside the numerous and deeply embedded marks of dependence on the Old Greek the Psalms of Solomon sporadically exhibit readings drawn from a revised Septuagint. Although to the best of my knowledge these readings had not hitherto been recognized for what they are, their presence in the Psalms of Solomon should not be a cause of great surprise. A prominent strand of Septuagint scholarship over the last seventy years or so has been constructed around the idea that revisionary activity of the *kaige*-type was located in Palestine, and that it set in before the middle of the first century BCE.[47] Our findings in the Psalms of Solomon confirm this picture.

The name of Theodotion is attached to one of the revisions of the Septuagint that Origen included in his Hexapla around the middle of the third century. Most of the Hexapla itself is lost forever, but patristic testimonies and marginal notes in Septuagint manuscripts preserve many readings attributed to "the Three": Aquila, Symmachus, Theodotion. These minor versions revise, each according to its own principles, the Old Greek so as to make it adhere more closely to a Masoretic-type Hebrew text. Traditionally, these versions have been understood as the work of individuals who lived in the second century CE. Remarks of Irenaeus and Epiphanius have led scholars to date Theodotion's *floruit* toward the end of the second century CE, during the reign of Commodus, between 180 and 192 CE. This date would put Theodotion sometime after Aquila and Symmachus. But it raises two questions. Typologically, Theodotion is a sort of half-way house between the Septuagint and Aquila: more literal than the former but less so than the latter. It would make sense to situate the revision before Aquila (*ca.* 120 CE) rather than after. More pointedly, readings attributed to Theodotion turn up already in first-century sources, notably the writings of Flavius Josephus and the New Testament.[48]

---

47 See Jan Joosten, "New light on Proto-Theodotion. The Psalms of Solomon and the Milieu of the *Kaige* Recension," in *Die Septuaginta – Geschichte, Wirkung, Relevanz,* ed. Martin Meiser et al., WUNT 405 (Tübingen: Mohr Siebeck, 2018), 304–315.

48 See See Emil Schürer, *Geschichte des jüdischen Volkes im Zeitalter Jesu Christi,* III (Leipzig: Hinrichs, 1898$^3$), 323–324; see also Swete, *Introduction*, 47–48.

These considerations have led to the idea that Theodotion may have to be dated much earlier than the patristic evidence indicates. Alternatively, the late-second-century Theodotion may have used an earlier revision, adopting many of its readings.

In the nineteen fifties and sixties, Dominique Barthélemy gave an important boost to the concept of proto-Theodotion. Building on the work of Henry Thackeray, he showed that distinct marks of Theodotion's translation technique were attested in important sections of what is usually regarded as the Septuagint, notably the books of Ruth, Lamentations and Song of Songs, and parts of the books of Kingdoms.[49] On the basis of one peculiar feature he named these texts the "*kaige* group." He also demonstrated that the Greek version of the Minor Prophets found in the Judean desert in the nineteen fifties (8HevXIIgr) exhibits some of the same marks. Stretches of a text very closely aligned with this witness are quoted by Justin Martyr, who died *circa* 165 CE, thus proving that the revision precedes Theodotion as traditionally dated. The paleography of the manuscript of 8HevXII gr points to an earlier date still. Based on these data, Barthélemy argued that Theodotion had to be dated to the first century CE and should be regarded as a precursor, a *devancier*, of Aquila. He located the revision in Palestine and argued that it originated in Rabbinic circles.[50]

Barthélemy's views on the *kaige* group have been widely accepted, though with important modifications. Notably the date of the Minor Prophets scroll from Nahal Hever is now thought to be first century BCE, as argued by Peter Parsons on paleographic grounds.[51] Most knowledgeable scholars agree that the scroll attests a revision of the Septuagint along the lines of Theodotion, thus proving that revisions of this type were already underway in the early Roman period. The ultra-literal translation of Aquila did not drop from the clear sky in the second century CE, but incorporated the work of generations of scholars who perfected this particular art. The fact that the scroll was

49 Barthélemy, *Devanciers.*

50 Barthélemy identified Theodotion with Jonathan ben Uzziel to whom the Targum of the Prophets is traditionally attributed. At the same time he insists on the diversity of the writings exhibiting "Theodotionic" hallmarks: not all the writings can be the work of the same author.

51 See Peter J. Parsons in E. Tov, *The Greek Minor Prophets Scroll from Nahal Hever (8HevXIIgr)* DJD 8 (Oxford: Clarendon Press, 1990), 19–38.

found in the Judean desert does not conclusively prove that the text it contains was produced in the homeland, but it makes it likely. General considerations also point in this direction: circles in Judea would have had both the motivation and the ability to carry out a revision of the Greek version on the basis of a Hebrew model.

In light of these considerations, the presence of readings attested for Theodotion or Aquila, or conforming to the translational profile of the *kaige*-Theodotion group, in the Psalms of Solomon stands to reason. The community among which the songs were composed read the scriptures in the Septuagint version, but by the time they wrote the songs, their text of the Septuagint had absorbed a number readings that originated in revised texts circulating in Palestine.

This presence of *kaige*-type readings in the Psalms of Solomon has important ramifications for the textual history of the Septuagint. A well-known problem in Septuagint studies is that most witnesses to the Greek text are contaminated with readings corrected on the basis of a proto-Masoretic Hebrew source text. A massive source of contamination is Origen's Hexapla. But many considerations lead scholars to think that the contamination did not start with the Hexapla. Scriptural allusions in the Psalms of Solomon allow us a glimpse of what the text of the Septuagint may have looked like in Jerusalem during the second half of the first century BCE. Through a type of textual osmosis with revisions of the *kaige* type—the two text types being copied, read, studied and celebrated side-by-side in the same locale—the Septuagint itself grew closer to the proto-Masoretic Hebrew text. Although the material is too scant to provide precise information on individual readings, it offers a precious snapshot of textual evolution in this relatively early time frame.

## 5.6. The congregation of the devout and the *kaige*-group: a thought experiment

The authors of the Psalms of Solomon and the *kaige*-group would seem to have been active in or near Jerusalem in the same time frame. As was shown in chapter 4, they share a number of scriptural readings as well as some rare items of vocabulary. One might be tempted to identify the two groups. This temptation is to be resisted, however. Some of the allusions in the Psalms of Solomon involve Septuagint readings that diverge wildly from the Masoretic text; this would not be expected of bilingual scribes whose day-job was to assimilate the Old Greek to the received Hebrew. The devout who wrote the songs and the scribes who corrected the Greek text of scripture belonged to distinct circles. Nevertheless, some characteristics are common to both. A comparison will prove worthwhile even if it requires some scholarly imagination to fill in a few gaps.

**Immigrants from the western diaspora**

Both groups had good, and probably native, command of Greek and both read the Septuagint as scripture.

For the community of the Psalms of Solomon I have argued that the use of Greek reflects a connection to the western diaspora (see above in 5.2 and 5.3). Although they were settled in Jerusalem, and identified deeply with the city in all its vicissitudes, they were in all likelihood descendants of Jews from the diaspora who had moved to Jerusalem. In light of the eschatological tenor of Sol 17, their "return to Zion" may well have had a religious motivation. Their origin in the diaspora accounts not only for their use of Greek in worship and theology, but also for other peculiarities, notably their somewhat disincarnate relation to the Jerusalem Temple. The authors and their target audience were Jews and Jerusalemites, yet they maintained certain habits and beliefs that had been imported from abroad.

A similar background may be suspected for the revisors.[52] The motivation and the ability to carry out a revision may reflect the Judean context (see section 5.4), but the use of Greek in religious writing reflects the habits of the diaspora. So does the attachment to the Septuagint. The revisors were intimately familiar with the translation, often drawing the material for their revision from other passages in the Old Greek. We don't know where exactly the *kaige*-group was localized, although Jerusalem is a fair guess. Nor do we have information on the motivation of their return to the home land. One might think they moved there in order to revise the Septuagint. But it may well be

52 See Anneli Aejmelaeus, "The Origins of the *Kaige* Revision," in *Scriptures in the Making: Texts and Their Transmission in Late Second Temple Judaism*, ed. Raimo Hakola, Paavo Huotari, Jessi Orpana, CBET 109 (Leuven: Peeters, 2022), 285–311

that the idea to revise took shape in Palestine. In the diaspora, there would hardly have been a need for it. The Letter of Aristeas, written no doubt some time before the Nahal Hever Minor Prophets scroll, actively militates against the idea of revision.[53] A century later, Philo is still perfectly happy to think that the Greek Torah and its Hebrew source text are nearly identical—an idea he could only hold because he knew no Hebrew, or very little.[54] The attitude of the *kaige* group is different: unlike Philo, they are aware of the differences between the Septuagint and the received Hebrew, and unlike Aristeas, they accept that something needs to be done about them. The impetus for these views emerged at the interface between Jews of the diaspora and Jews of the homeland.

**Avid readers of scripture and of Psalms in particular**

Both circles were heavily invested in scriptural interpretation, although in different settings. The authors of the Psalms of Solomon used scripture with a view to edifying their community through liturgy. The revisors aimed at producing a more accurate Greek version than had been available before—more accurate according to their criteria.

No special focus on the Pentateuch can be observed among either group. The songs quote a wide variety of scriptural writings (chapter 1) and the revision, too, is known to have been applied to many parts of scripture. If there is a focal point in the scriptural activity of the two groups it is the book of Psalms. For the Psalms of Solomon this feature has been discussed in chapter 2.[55] The titles of the songs, their poetic form and vocabulary, and the way they reference scriptural motifs are all reminiscent of Psalms. This shows that for the group, Psalms stood out as a dominant corpus in their liturgical practice and their piety.

53 See Sebastian Brock, "To Revise or not to Revise: Attitudes to Jewish Biblical Translation," in *Septuagint, Scrolls and Cognate Writings (Manchester 1990)*, ed. George J. Brooke and Barnabas Lindars, SCS 33 (Atlanta: Scholars Press, 1992), 301–338.

54 See *Life of Moses* 2:37.

55 See notably sections 2.4 and 2.5.

The *kaige*-group also manifests specific closeness to Psalms.[56] Several scholars have pointed out that some striking translation equivalents characterizing the *kaige*-group started out as innovations of the Septuagint of Psalms.

- In Psalm 98/97:6, where two words for trumpet, שופר and חצצרה, both of them usually translated as σάλπιγξ, occur side by side, the Septuagint differentiates the two as σάλπιγξ ἐλατή "metal trumpet" and σάλπιγξ κερατίνη "horn trumpet."[57] The *kaige*-group, apparently taking its cue from this verse, renders שופר rather systematically as κερατίνη—a substantivized use of the adjective without parallel elsewhere in Greek—and חצצרה as σάλπιγξ.[58]
- The expression "Lord of Hosts" (יהוה צבאות), is usually translated as κύριος Σαβαωθ or κύριος παντοκράτωρ, but in Psalms it is most often rendered, more literally, as κύριος τῶν δυνάμεων. The *kaige*-group adopts the latter equivalent and uses it consistently.[59]
- In Psalm 7:12 the translators had to render both אלהים and אל, both usually translated with θεός "God," in the same verse. The creative solution they came up with was to translate אל as an adjective, ἰσχυρός, "strong." The *kaige*-group uses ἰσχυρός systematically to render Hebrew אל "God."[60]

Evidence like this suggest that the revisers of the *kaige*-group had studied the Psalter in Greek and Hebrew and lent authority to its translation technique.[61] Although they revered many other books, their

56 See Barthélemy, *Devanciers*, 47 (tentatively); Olivier Munnich, "La Septante des Psaumes et le groupe *kaige*," *VT* 33 (1983), 75–89; S. Olofsson, "The Kaige Group and the Septuagint Book of Psalms," in *IX Congress of the International Organization for Septuagint and Cognate Studies: Cambridge 1995*, ed. Bernard A. Taylor (Atlanta: Scholars, 1997), 189–230; Peter J. Gentry, "The Greek Psalter and the καίγε Tradition," in *The Old Greek Psalter*, ed. R.J.V. Hiebert, C. E. Cox, and P. J. Gentry (Sheffield: Academic Press, 2001), 74–97.

57 The Psalms translator partly draws upon Num 10:2 for the first of these renderings.

58 Barthélemy, *Devanciers*, 61–62.

59 Barthélemy, *Devanciers*, 82–83.

60 Barthélemy, *Devanciers*, 83.

61 An additional example is pointed out in Jan Joosten, "The verb συνετίζω 'to instruct' in the Septuagint Psalms and beyond" in *"Må de nu förklara..." Om bibeltexter, religion, litteratur. Festskrift för Staffan Olofsson*, ed.

attachment to Psalms stands out. In this they resemble the authors of the Psalms of Solomon.

If this common devotion to Greek Psalms is not due to accident, it must have its roots in the diaspora. Admittedly, we could not have guessed from reading Philo that the Psalms were particularly popular in Greek-speaking synagogues.[62] But perhaps in this case Philo is the odd man out.

**Similar but not identical**

The authors of the Psalms of Solomon and the *kaige*-revisers are Jewish groups with a diasporic background who had settled in Judea and adapted to the Judaism of the homeland in several respects. Although they belong to the same period, they do not represent the same group. Several allusions in the Psalms of Solomon diverge from the Masoretic form of the passage in question to an extent that would presumably have made a *kaige*-reviser wince.

The presence of *kaige*-like readings in the Psalms of Solomon does not prove that the two groups were in touch, but it seems likely that they were. Occasional contacts would account well for the traces of a revised text of scripture in the Psalms of Solomon.

## 5.7. The openness to new ideas circulating in the homeland

While retaining certain habits of the diaspora—notably the use of Greek in religious discourse—the authors of the Psalms of Solomon were also subject to local conditions. The influence is sufficiently conspicuous to suggest a readiness to embrace views circulating among Judean Jews. In all likelihood the returnees considered the religious teaching of schools in the homeland authoritative. They would have

Rosmari Lillas-Schuil et al. (Göteborg: LIR, 2018), 105–113. A systematic search for other instances would likely be fruitful.

62 See Ralph Brucker, "Observations on the *Wirkungsgeschichte* of the Septuagint-Psalms in Ancient Judaism and Early Christianity," *in: Septuagint Research. Issues and Challenges in the Study of the Greek Jewish Scriptures*, ed. Wolfgang Kraus and R. Glenn Wooden, SBLSCS 53 (Atlanta: SBL/Leiden: Brill, 2006), 355–369.

subscribed to the words of Isaiah: "For out of Zion shall go forth instruction" (Isa 2:3).[63]

The imprint of Rabbinic or proto-Rabbinic ideas on the Psalms of Solomon has led many scholars to view them as a product of the Pharisees.[64] In Sol 9:3–4 the juxtaposition of statements on divine omniscience and human free will is strongly reminiscent of Mishna Aboth 3:15, "All is foreseen, but freedom of choice is given."[65] Another point of doctrine in which the songs agree with the Pharisees is the belief in resurrection and distinct forms of afterlife for the righteous and the wicked (Sol 3:11–12; 14: 9–10).[66] Some of the terminology used to express this doctrine finds striking parallels in Rabbinic writings. Notably, the noun κληρονομία "inheritance" and the verb κληρονομέω "to inherit" when applied to conditions in the afterlife adumbrate Rabbinic usage:

> **Sol 14:9**[67]
> Therefore their (the sinners') inheritance is Hades and darkness and destruction,

This may be the earliest attestation of a mode of expression that is extremely frequent in Rabbinic writings.[68]

---

63 Because the views in question are roughly speaking of a Pharisaic-Rabbinic nature, our enquiry finds itself confronted with a well-known problem of method: practically all the sources for said views are much later than the Psalms of Solomon. We will proceed on the understanding, which is widely—though not universally—shared among specialists of Rabbinic literature, that those sources transmit early traditions, some of which go back to the first century BCE or even before. For an eloquent defense of this approach, see Michel Remaud, *Évangile et tradition rabbinique* (Bruxelles: Lessius, 2003), 17–30.

64 In recent times, this view has admittedly lost some of its popularity.

65 Compare Josephus, *Antiq.* 18:13 "when they [the Pharisees] determine that all things are done by fate, they do not take away the freedom from men of acting as they think fit"; similarly *War* 2:162–163.

66 Compare *Antiq.* 18:14; *War* 2:164; for Rabbinic Judaism, see Hermann L. Strack, Paul Billerbeck, *Kommentar zum Neuen testament aus Talmud und Midrasch*, IV 2 (München: Beck, 1928), 1166–1198.

67 See also Sol 14:10; 15:10.

68 See Strack-Billerbeck I (1926), 829.

More speculatively, the beginning of Sol 14 may contain an allusion to "paradise" ("the garden of Eden") as the post-death destination of the righteous:

**Sol 14:3–4**
The devout of the Lord shall live by it (the law) forever;
the orchard (παράδεισος) of the Lord, the trees of life, are his devout.
Their planting is rooted forever; they shall not be pulled up all the days of heaven.

The pairing of the "garden of the Lord"[69] with the "trees of life" clearly references the second creation story in Gen 2–3.[70] The threefold insistence on eternal duration as well as the context in Sol 14 suggest that the passage speaks of the afterlife. The identification of the devout as the trees of life is somewhat peculiar,[71] but the implication is still that the devout will end up in the "garden" (παράδεισος) of the Lord, i.e. in Paradise. Thus, the verse would seem to be an early attestation of the notion that the righteous after their death will live forever in the garden of Eden. Unless I err, this motif is not found in other Second-Temple literature. It next turns up in writings of the late first century CE—the New Testament, 4 Ezra and Syriac Baruch—and then recurs very often in Rabbinic writings.[72]

The terminological features—"to inherit" hell (or eternal life), and "paradise" as the destiny of the righteous—are not attested in the Hebrew Bible, nor in the Septuagint, but they do occur much later, in Hebrew, in Rabbinic writings. It is a credible hypothesis that these expressions came to the authors of the Psalms of Solomon from the Judaism of their surroundings.

---

69 See Gen 2–3; Isa 51:3; Gen 13:10; Ezek 28:13; and cf. Rev 2:7.

70 The allusion was not included in the list of chapter 1 because it does not refer to a specific passage, but to an entire chapter.

71 The figure of the righteous as a tree may owe something to Psalm 1:3, see Sven Behnke, *Psalm Salomo 14 Text, Tradition und Komposition einer frühjüdischen Dichtung*, Beiträge zur Erforschung des Alten Testaments und des Antiken Judentums, 64 (Berlin: Peter Lang, 2021). A similar conjunction of motifs, with the righteous represented in the image of trees in the garden of Eden is found in the Hymns Scroll, 1QHa 16:6–7. See also the Odes of Solomon 11:16–24.

72 See notably Luke 23:43; Strack-Billerbeck II, 265; IV 2, 1016–1065.

The conclusion that the authors were Pharisees does not follow. Alongside the resemblances, there are notable differences. In section 5.2, we noted the relative lack of importance of sacrifice for the authors of the Psalms of Solomon, a trait that probably differentiated them from Pharisaic circles.[73] We should also observe that, in spite of the strong interest in divine education, the notion of studying the Torah is never in the foreground in the Psalms of Solomon. The authors are not Pharisees, but like other inhabitants of Judea in the first century BCE they have been exposed to their influence and have absorbed some of their teaching.[74]

## 5.8. Concluding reflections

In this final chapter I have tried to identify two distinct bodies of tradition that left a mark on the Psalms of Solomon. The authors, I argue, drew on ideas that circulated among Greek-speaking Jews in the dispersion. At the same time, they were open to the new religious ferment circulating in the homeland. This striking combination reflects their historical situation. The authors, it seems, belonged to a group of Jews who had returned from the diaspora to the homeland or, more likely, to the descendants of such a group.

The use of the Greek language and the constant reference to the Greek version of scripture in the Psalms of Solomon point to a connection with the western diaspora. This connection accounts for patterns of thought and expression echoing the religious culture of Greek-speaking Judaism (sections 5.2 to 5.4). Although the anthological

73 See above, note 20.

74 The *kaige*-group too has been viewed as belonging to the Pharisaic-Rabbinic current of Judaism, and by none other than Barthélemy. In the first chapter of the *Devanciers*, Barthélemy tries to demonstrate that the translation technique of Aquila is rooted in the hermeneutics of Rabbi Akiba, while the approach of the *kaige*-group reflects the more conservative hermeneutics of earlier Rabbis. It is fair to say, however, that this aspect of Barthélemy' work is the one that has resisted the least in the face of scholarly criticism. For the discussion, see e.g. Leonard J. Greenspoon, "Recensions, Revision, Rabbinics: Dominique Barthélemy and Early Developments in the Greek Traditions," *Textus* 15 (1990), 153–167.

style and recurrent themes recall the Qumran Hodayot, the way the authors express their central concerns specifically resembles Greek texts: the Septuagint, in both its translated and non-translated books, and para-biblical literature standing close to the Septuagint. The level of Greek education of the authors of the Psalms of Solomon is not comparable to that of Philo or the author of Wisdom of Solomon, but the cultural reservoir into which they dip is the same. Only a small part of the relevant material could be presented in the present study, and much work remains to be done in this perspective.[75]

Alongside the traditions of the western diaspora, however, a second source of influence is to be recognized, namely Pharisaic/proto-Rabbinic Judaism as it was shaping up in Judea during the first century BCE (sections 5.5 to 5.7). The authors of the Psalms of Solomon took note of the new teaching developed within this group, and adopted parts of it that were congenial to their own religious experience.

In comparison to Septuagintal writings, Psalms of Solomon is a relative late-comer. In contrast, in the proto-Rabbinic tradition, Psalms of Solomon stands out as a very early witness, in several instances containing the first attestation of notions and motifs exemplifying this stream.[76]

Although the history of traditions does not lend itself to easy quantification, the proportion of Septuagint versus non-Septuagint—or rather: not exclusively Septuagint—allusions in the Psalms of Solomon is suggestive. Out of 50 relatively certain allusions, only 8 meaningfully align with a non-Septuagintal version or translation technique (chapters 3 and 4). This ratio would seem to be a reasonable reflection of the formative influences that can be recognized in the corpus: the predominant traits have roots in the western diaspora (sections 5.2 to 5.4), while a minor set of motifs and theologoumena can be traced back to Palestinian Judaism of the early Roman period (section 5.5 to 5.7).

75 The two studies of Eberhard Bons quoted in note 11 illustrate the type of results that may be attained in a patient approach of the corpus as a Greek writing.

76 This was correctly perceived by Julius Wellhausen. Wellhausen erred, however, in concluding that the Psalms of Solomon were themselves a Pharisaic work.

Retracing the origin of cultural influences in an ancient writing is delicate. Religious milieus and traditions are not watertight. There was a lot of Hellenism in Judea, and Pharisaic/proto-Rabbinic teaching naturally spread to the Greek-speaking diaspora as well.[77] Moreover, one should not lose sight of the fact that much of the content of the Psalms of Solomon goes back to much earlier phases in Judaism. The historical reconstructions proposed in this chapter must therefore remain hypothetical and approximative. Nevertheless, the bi-faced nature of the corpus as such would seem to be sufficiently well established. It is what lends the Psalms of Solomon their unique profile.

77 Paul of Tarsus, whose native language was Greek and whose scripture—as far as we can tell from his letters—was the Septuagint, regarded himself as a Pharisee and studied the oral law in Jerusalem.

# Conclusions and Perspectives

To the authors of the Psalms of Solomon, allusions to scripture were a means to attain their rhetorical aims. To modern-day researchers the allusions provide clues to the historical context of the authors. On the basis of some 50 allusions collected in chapter 1, chapter 2 investigates aspects of the dynamics of Psalms of Solomon's rhetoric. The authors of the corpus present themselves as writers of psalms in continuation of the Davidic psalter. The piety and the ethics they argue for are presented in scriptural terms, and—more strikingly—so are historical events and conditions of mid-first century BCE Jerusalem.

The next two chapters explore what the allusions can tell us of the history and identity of the group that produced the corpus. A crucial insight is that the Septuagintal wording of the allusions must be native. In several instances, only the Greek version of the passage alluded to—not any Hebrew text form—can serve the authors' argument. This implies that the Psalms of Solomon were originally created in Greek. At first, this observation appears to clash with what else is known about the corpus: why would a Jewish group in first-century BCE Jerusalem write religious poetry in Greek? And for whom? On reflection, however, the language of composition turns out to be in tune with other aspects that have recently been highlighted. The theme of exile and dispersion is very present throughout the corpus. Some turns of phrase witness to a "diasporic worldview." Things fall into place when we admit that the Psalms of Solomon may be the product of a group of Jews from the western diaspora who had migrated back to the home country.

An additional insight gains in relevance at this point. In a small number of allusions, the Greek wording does not seem to echo the Septuagint but stands closer to the traditional Hebrew text. These divergences from the Old Greek agree partly with later revisions of the Septuagint, notably with the diffuse group going under the name of *kaige*-Theodotion. In the homeland, the Septuagint text read and transmitted within the group that produced our corpus was partially reworked so as to agree with the emerging Masoretic text. The earliest representative of the *kaige* group, the Greek Minor Prophets scroll from Nahal Hever, dates to the middle of the first century BCE and is thus approximately contemporary with the Psalms of Solomon.

Two facets come to light in the analysis of Psalms of Solomon's allusions to scripture: the text alluded to is the Septuagint, partly revised on the basis of the received Hebrew text. The use of the Septuagint, including some phrases that were never part of the Hebrew Bible, points to the diasporic origin of the group. The signs of revision witness to the group's location in the homeland. The last chapter tentatively illustrates how these two facets come to light in ideas and themes developed in Psalms of Solomon. In several instances, the thought and the terminology link up with the Septuagint specifically, while elsewhere we find imagery and theologoumena characteristic of Palestinian Judaism.

# Appendix: Sol 11:2–7 and Bar 4:36–5:9

As Eduard Ephraem Geiger was the first to realize, the body of Sol 11 has a precise and extensive parallel in the last part of the book of Baruch.[1] A synopsis of Bar 5:1, 5–8 and Sol 11:2–7 will show the extent of the similarity:[2]

| **Bar 5** | **Sol 11** |
|---|---|
| 1 Take off your robe of mourning and affliction, O Ierousalem,<br>and **put on** the dignity of **the glory** from God forever. | |
| 5 Arise, O Ierousalem, and **stand upon the height**,<br>and look around toward the east, and **see your children gathered** from the setting of the sun until its rising at the word of the Holy One, rejoicing at God's remembering. | 2 **Stand upon a high place**, O Ierousalem, and **see your children**, from the east and the west, **gathered** together once again by the Lord.<br>3 From the north they come in the joy of their God;<br>from the islands far away God has gathered them |
| 6 For they went out from you on foot, led away by enemies,<br>but God will bring them to you, taken up with glory, as on a royal throne. | |
| 7 For God has instructed that every **high mountain** and the everlasting mounds be **made low** and the valleys be filled to make **level** the ground so that Israel may walk safely by the glory of God. | 4 He has **made low high mountains** into **level** ground for them;<br>the hills fled at their approach. |
| 8 And even **the woods and every tree of fragrance have shaded** Israel at God's ordinance. | 5 **The woods shaded** them as they passed by;<br>God caused **every tree of fragrance** to spring up for them,<br>6 that Israel might pass by at the visitation of their God's glory. |

1 Eduard Ephraem Geiger, *Der Psalter Salomo's erklärt und herausgegeben* (Augsburg: Wolffisch, 1871), 137.

2 The NETS translation has been slightly adapted to bring out verbal parallels between the two texts.

7 **Put on**, O Ierousalem, the garments of your **glory**;
prepare the robe of your sanctity,
for God has spoken good concerning Israel forever and ever.

In Baruch, the apostrophe to Jerusalem goes from 4:30 to 5:9, but other than the verses quoted above only verses 36–37, which partly anticipate 5:5, have elements in common with Sol 11. Conversely, the outer frame of Sol 11, verses 1 and 8–9, does not contain any echoes of Baruch. Both passages address Jerusalem and predict the return of the exiles.

Much scholarly acuity has been expended on defining the relation between Sol 11 and Bar 4:36–5:9.[3] Establishing the direction of dependence has proved difficult. Geiger took the parallel to mean that Sol 11 depended on Baruch. In his view, the author who composed the Psalms of Solomon in Hebrew followed the model of a Hebrew version of Baruch. This was not a necessary conclusion. Ryle and James, whose extensive discussion of the parallel has been very influential, argued instead that Baruch depended on Sol 11. In their view, this part of Baruch was created in Greek on the basis of the Greek translation of Sol 11, after the destruction of the Temple in 70 CE.[4] A third approach, formulated by Kneucker in his commentary on Baruch and adopted by Viteau, is that the parallel came into being by accident because the two passages related to the same collection of prophecies in Isaiah 40–66.[5] Finally, some scholars have argued that the two texts depend on a third one, which has not been preserved.[6]

The nature of the connection between the two passages is doubly relevant to our investigation. Firstly, because the parallel comprises

3 Erzberger has recently retraced the history of research in detail, see Johanna Erzberger, "Changing Contexts: Psalms of Solomon 11 and Its Parallel in Baruch 4:5–5:9," *The Psalms of Solomon: Texts, Contexts, and Intertexts*, ed. G. Antony Keddie, Patrick Pouchelle, Kenneth Atkinson, EJL 54 (Atlanta: SBL, 2021), 35–56. Other extensive discussions are W. Pesch, "Die Abhängigkeit des 11. Salomonischen Psalms vom letzten Kapitel des Buches Baruch," *ZAW* 67 (1955), 251–263; André Kabasele Mukenge, *L'unité du livre de Baruch* (Paris : Gabalda, 1998), 345–356.

4 Ryle and James, *Psalms of the Pharisees*, lxxii–lxxvii.

5 Viteau, *Psaumes de Salomon*, 149.

6 See notably Erzberger, "Changing Contexts," 41.

several allusions to passages in Isaiah, it potentially complicates some of the claims made in chapters 1 and 4. If Baruch were the earlier writing, the allusions in Sol to Isa 60:4 and 52:1 would on the face of it be indirect. Secondly, if Baruch were the earlier writing, then the parallel would in all likelihood have to be regarded as an allusion to scripture. The extensive reference to Baruch would indicate that the book formed part of the scriptures read and venerated among the group that produced the Psalms of Solomon.

In the present appendix, I will not pretend to solve the question of priority, but merely discuss some issues of relevance to the present monograph.

## Verbal overlap

As the bolded words in the above synopsis show, much of the wording of the two passages is identical or nearly identical. The similarity is as impressive in Greek as it is in the English translation:

Bar 5:1 **ἔνδυσαι** τὴν εὐπρέπειαν **τῆς** παρὰ τοῦ θεοῦ **δόξης**

Sol 11:7 **Ἔνδυσαι**, Ιερουσαλημ, τὰ ἱμάτια **τῆς δόξης** σου

Bar 5:5 ἀνάστηθι, **Ιερουσαλημ**, καὶ **στῆθι ἐπὶ** τοῦ **ὑψηλοῦ**

Sol 11:2 **στῆθι, Ιερουσαλημ, ἐφ'** ὑψηλοῦ

Bar 5:5 **καὶ ἰδέ σου συνηγμένα τὰ τέκνα ἀπὸ** ἡλίου **δυσμῶν** ἕως **ἀνατολῶν**

Sol 11:2 **καὶ ἰδὲ τὰ τέκνα σου ἀπὸ ἀνατολῶν καὶ δυσμῶν συνηγμένα**

Bar 5:7 συνέταξεν γὰρ ὁ θεὸς **ταπεινοῦσθαι** πᾶν **ὄρος ὑψηλὸν** καὶ θῖνας ἀενάους καὶ φάραγγας πληροῦσθαι **εἰς ὁμαλισμὸν τῆς γῆς**

Sol 11:4 **ὄρη ὑψηλὰ ἐταπείνωσεν εἰς ὁμαλισμὸν αὐτοῖς**

Bar 5:8 **ἐσκίασαν** δὲ καὶ **οἱ δρυμοὶ** καὶ **πᾶν ξύλον εὐωδίας** τῷ Ισραηλ προστάγματι τοῦ θεοῦ

Sol 11:5 **οἱ δρυμοὶ ἐσκίασαν** αὐτοῖς ἐν τῇ παρόδῳ αὐτῶν, **πᾶν ξύλον εὐωδίας** ἀνέτειλεν αὐτοῖς ὁ θεός

The common wording overlaps with shared allusions to Isaiah, as might be expected. Even in the allusions, however, the two texts exhibit common features that diverge from the Isaianic text:

Bar 5:7 πᾶν ὄρος **ὑψηλόν**; Sol 11:4 ὄρη **ὑψηλά**

Isa 40:4 πᾶν ὄρος

Bar 5:7 ; Sol 11:4 **εἰς ὁμαλισμόν**

Isa 45:2 **ὁμαλιῶ** "I will make level"

Moreover, the verbal overlap extends to passages that have no scriptural model. Notably in Bar 5:8 and Sol 11:5 the motif of the woods and the "trees of fragrance" shading the Israelites during their voyage, which is not found in any other writing we know, is expressed in the same words (οἱ δρυμοί, ἐσκίασαν, πᾶν ξύλον εὐωδίας).[7]

The extent to which our two passages share the same language makes some type of contact a near certainty. Either Sol 11 draws on Bar 5, or Bar 5 on Sol 11, or both passages follow the model of a third text that has not been preserved. The notion that the similarities between Sol 11 and Bar 5 are due to their relating to the same set of intertexts from Isaiah cannot be sustained.

The extent of the common wording also strongly indicates that the contact happened in Greek. For the allusions, one might argue that the wording was suggested by the Septuagint. But the verbal overlap also happens in passages not based on scripture. The conclusion is unescapable: the intertextual process took place in Greek.[8]

## Intertexts from Isaiah

Both texts consist of a string of allusions to verses in Isaiah:

- Isa 52:1 in Bar 5:1; Sol 11:7
- Isa 60:4 in Bar 5:5; Sol 11:2
- Isa 45:2 in Bar 5:7; Sol 11:4
- Isa 40:4 in Bar 5:7; Sol 11:4[9]

The first allusion in this list is placed before the other three in Bar 5, but after them in Sol 11. Otherwise, the references occur in the same

7 Note also the parallels between Bar 5:5 and Sol 11:2, which have no direct model in Isaiah (but cf. Isa 40:9): στῆθι, ἐπὶ, ὑψηλοῦ.

8 Erzberger, "Changing Contexts"; see also Geza Xeravits, *"Take Courage, O Jerusalem..." Studies in the Psalms of Baruch 4–5* (Deuterocanonical and Cognate Literature Studies, 25; Berlin: De Gruyter 2015), 121–125.

9 Only the first two examples were considered strong enough to be included in the list in chapter 1.

order in the two texts. The reference to the same Isaianic verses, partly in the same order, again shows that the similarity between Bar 5 and Sol 11 should not be attributed to chance, but to some form of direct dependence.

A comparison of the Isaianic passages with the allusions brings to light some interesting data:

> Isa 52:1
> ἔνδυσαι τὴν ἰσχύν σου, Σιων, καὶ ἔνδυσαι τὴν δόξαν σου Ιερουσαλημ
> Put on your strength, O Sion, and put on your glory, O Ierousalem

As was observed in chapter 4, there is a divergence between the Septuagint ("put on your glory") and the Masoretic text ("put on your glorious garments"). Sol 11:7 goes with the MT, probably following a revised Septuagint, as was argued in chapter 4. Bar 5:1, however, seems to reflect the Old Greek: "put on the dignity of the glory from God forever." Although this is paraphrastic, the base text seems to be the Septuagint. There is no reference to the MT's garments.

> Isa 60:4
> ἆρον κύκλῳ τοὺς ὀφθαλμούς σου καὶ ἰδὲ συνηγμένα τὰ τέκνα σου
> Lift up your eyes round about, and see your children gathered together

Here both Bar 5 and Sol 11 follow the Septuagint specifically, while the Hebrew text does not mention the children at this point (see chapter 1). Baruch takes a bit more from the intertext than Sol 11: Bar 5:5 "look around" (περίβλεψαι) seems to be a free variation on the Septuagint's "lift up your eyes round about." Note also that for the part the two texts have in common, the word order in Bar 5:5 stands closer to the intertext than in Sol 11:4.

> Isa 40:4
> πᾶσα φάραγξ πληρωθήσεται καὶ πᾶν ὄρος καὶ βουνὸς ταπεινωθήσεται
> Every ravine shall be filled up, and every mountain and hill be made low

Here again, Bar 5 ("and the valleys be filled") takes more from Isaiah than Sol 11.

Isa 45:2
Εγὼ ἔμπροσθέν σου πορεύσομαι καὶ ὄρη ὁμαλιῶ
I will go before you and level mountains

This verse probably lies at the basis of the expression εἰς ὁμαλισμόν "for levelling" in Bar 5:7 and Sol 11:4. The MT here does not refer to mountains but to הֲדוּרִים, the meaning of which is debated.[10] The association of Isa 45:2 with 40:4 reflects the Septuagint specifically.

Taking the four cases together, there can be little doubt that the textual source of the allusions our two texts have in common is the Septuagint. The vocabulary shows this, as well as the divergent readings in the allusions to Isa 60:4 and 45:2. This conclusion confirms that the textual process leading to the parallel between Bar 5 and Sol 11 happened in Greek.

In addition, the analysis suggests that, whatever the direction of dependence, the author who borrowed also consulted the Isaianic intertexts directly.

If a supplementer added Bar 4:36–5:9 at the end of the book on the basis of Sol 11, as argued by Ryle and James, the additional elements from Isa 60:4 and 40:4 pointed out above ("look around" and "and the valleys be filled") must have been added from the text of Isaiah. Such independent recourse to the intertexts would not be at all surprising. The texts in question were well known and quoted frequently in other writings as well.[11] The supplementer would have had little trouble finding them in his scriptures. He may even have known them well enough to add them from memory.

If the author of Sol 11 borrowed from Baruch, he left out several elements from the scriptural allusions in his textual model. This would have been done for poetic reasons—the verses in Baruch are very long and wordy, while in Sol 11 they are more concise. However, in at least one case, the author of Sol 11 must also have gone back to "his" text of Isaiah. In the allusion to Isa 52:1, he added "garments (of glory)." As argued in chapter 4, this element was probably taken from a revised

10 Note that 1QIsa[a] reads הררים "mountains," thus showing that the reading "mountains" was attested in Hebrew.

11 See Chad Reeser, "The Use of Isaiah in Psalm of Solomon 11 and Mark 1:1-15," draft paper published on Academia.edu.

text of Septuagint, of which other traces can be recognized in the Psalms of Solomon.[12]

In either scenario, the later writer would have acted as an author, freely reshaping his source text according to his own literary and theological purposes. It is to be expected of such an author that he would both add and subtract from the source text, and modify it in other ways too. Postulating an unattested common source from which Bar 5 and Sol 11 derive independently is a theoretical possibility, but as far as I can see it would not solve any philological problems. It is better to let the simpler hypothesis prevail, even if we don't know which one: either Baruch followed Solomon, or the reverse.

## Concluding (but inconclusive) reflections

If Bar 4:36–5:8 depended on Sol 11, it would be a unique witness to the early reception history of the Psalms of Solomon. But the parallel would have no implications for the meaning or the historical background of the Psalms of Solomon, nor, in particular, for its use of scripture.

As against this, if Sol 11 depended on Baruch, the parallel would be highly relevant to the topic of the present study. As a matter of fact, it would further strengthen some of the conclusions reached so far. Since the intertextual process appears to have happened in Greek, the case would provide additional proof that the Psalms of Solomon were originally composed in Greek. It would be nearly impossible to reconcile Sol 11's use of Baruch with the hypothesis of a Hebrew origin.

In this scenario, the example would also confirm that the Psalms of Solomon were composed in reference to the Greek version of Jewish scriptures. All the other allusions to scripture collected in chapter 1 are from books that ended up in the Rabbinic canon, but this would be a notable exception. Although Baruch may originally have been composed, wholly or partly, in Hebrew, it does not seem ever to have become authoritative in Hebrew/Aramaic-speaking Judaism. But Baruch is present in all versions of the Septuagint canon. Possibly, in

12 At the risk of suspending a mountain from a hair, the presence of a *kaige*-type reading in Sol's allusion to Isa 52:1 might incline the balance of probability in favor of the dependence of Sol 11 on Bar 5.

an early stage, the writing we call the book of Baruch was part of Greek Jeremiah.[13] This opens up an interesting possibility: if Sol 11 depends on Baruch 4:36–5:8, the author may have drawn his textual model from the Septuagint version of the book of Jeremiah. Either way, the use of Baruch would suggest, again, that the community that produced the Psalms of Solomon, while settled in Jerusalem, continued to observe certain habits of the diaspora.

The case would nevertheless be unique. Only in this instance would the author have modeled an entire psalm on a single textual model. In all other Psalms of Solomon, the intertextuality is far more eclectic. Only in this instance too would we find the "layered intertextuality" where scriptural allusions have two references—an immediate one, Baruch, and a more distant one, Isaiah.

In the present state of our knowledge, the impact of the parallel between Baruch and Sol 11 on our study remains limited. Uncertainty as to the direction of dependence makes it impossible to draw hard and fast conclusions.

13 See Pierre Bogaert, "Les frontières du canon de l'Ancien Testament dans l'Occident latin," in *La Bible juive dans l'Antiquité*, ed. Rémi Gounelle, Jan Joosten (Prahins: Zèbre, 2014), 41–95, in particular 75.

# Bibliography


Aejmelaeus, Anneli, "The Origins of the *Kaige* Revision," in *Scriptures in the Making: Texts and Their Transmission in Late Second Temple Judaism*, ed. Raimo Hakola, Paavo Huotari, Jessi Orpana, CBET 109 (Leuven: Peeters, 2022), 285–311.

Albrecht, Felix, *Psalmi Salomonis*, Septuaginta. Vetus Testamentum Graecum XII.3 (Göttingen: Vandenhoeck & Ruprecht, 2018).

*Aramaica Qumranica. Proceedings of the Conference on the Aramaic Texts from Qumran in Aix-en-Provence 30 June – 2 July 2008*, ed. Katell Berthelot, Daniel Stökl Ben Ezra (Leiden: Brill, 2010).

Arndt, William and F. Wilbur Gingrich, *A Greek-English Lexicon of the New Testament,* Second Edition Revised and Augmented by F. Wilbur Gingrich and Frederick Danker (Chicago: University of Chicago, 1979).

Atkinson, Kenneth, *An Intertextual Study of the Psalms of Solomon* (Lewiston NY: Edwin Mellen, 2001).

Atkinson, Kenneth, *I Cried to the Lord: A Study of the Psalms of Solomon's Historical Background and Social Setting*, SJSJ 84 (Leiden: Brill, 2013).

Barthélemy, Dominique, *Les devanciers d'Aquila : première publication intégrale du texte des fragments du dodécaprophéton trouvés dans le désert de Juda, précédée d'une étude sur les traductions et recensions grecques de la Bible réalisées au premier siècle de notre ère sous l'influence du rabbinat palestinien* (Leiden: Brill, 1963).

Behnke, Sven, *Psalm Salomo 14. Text, Tradition und Komposition einer frühjüdischen Dichtung*, Beiträge zur Erforschung des Alten Testaments und des Antiken Judentums, 64 (Berlin: Peter Lang, 2021).

Bezzel, Hannes, "„Und er schrieb Psalmen: dreitausendsechshundert" (11Q5, XXVII, 4f.). Psalmen-Bildung bei Ingo Baldermann im lichte von PsSal 5," in *Religion und Bildung – interdisziplinär. Festschrift für Michael Wermke zum 60. Geburtstag*, Studien zur

Religiösen Bildung 17 (Leipzig: Evangelische Verlagsanstalt, 2018), 25–36.

Bogaert, Pierre, "Les frontières du canon de l'Ancien Testament dans l'Occident latin," in *La Bible juive dans l'Antiquité*, ed. Rémi Gounelle, Jan Joosten (Prahins: Zèbre, 2014), 41–95.

Bons, Eberhard, "Philosophical Vocabulary in the Psalms of Solomon: The Case of Ps. Sol. 9:4," in *The Psalms of Solomon: Language, History, Theology*, ed. E. Bons, P. Pouchelle, Early Judaism and Its Literature 40 (Atlanta: SBL, 2015), 49–58.

Bons, Eberhard, "Psalms of Solomon 16:10 and Its Biblical and Hellenistic Backgrounds," in *The Psalms of Solomon: Texts, Contexts, and Intertexts*, ed. G. Antony Keddie, Patrick Pouchelle, Kenneth Atkinson, Early Judaism and Its Literature 54 (Atlanta: SBL, 2021), 23–33.

Brenton, Lancelot C. L. *The Septuagint with Apocrypha: Greek and English* (London: Bagster: 1851).

Brock, Sebastian, "To Revise or not to Revise: Attitudes to Jewish Biblical Translation," in *Septuagint, Scrolls and Cognate Writings (Manchester 1990)*, ed. George J. Brooke and Barnabas Lindars, SCS 33 (Atlanta: Scholars Press, 1992), 301–338.

Brucker, Ralph "Observations on the *Wirkungsgeschichte* of the Septuagint-Psalms in Ancient Judaism and Early Christianity," in *Septuagint Research. Issues and Challenges in the Study of the Greek Jewish Scriptures*, ed. Wolfgang Kraus and R. Glenn Wooden, SCS 53 (Atlanta: SBL/Leiden: Brill, 2006), 355–369.

Büchler, Adolph, *Types of Jewish-Palestinian Piety from 70 B.C.E. to 70 C.E. The Ancient Pious Men* (London: Jews' College, 1922).

Buth, Randall et al., "γίγας," in *Historical and Theological Lexicon of the Septuagint*, ed. Eberhard Bons (Tübingen: Mohr Siebeck, 2020), 1853–1864.

Ceulemans, Reinhart "Did Hesychius of Jerusalem Compose an Outline of the Sapiential Books (CPG 6560[4])?" in *Philologie, herméneutique et histoire des textes entre Orient et Occident: Mélanges en hommage à Sever J. Voicu*, ed. Francesca B. Barone et al. (Turnhout: Brepols, 2017), 343–380.

Collins, John, *The Scepter and the Star. Messianism in Light of the Dead Sea Scrolls* (Grand Rapids MI: Eerdmans, 2010$^{2}$).

Corley, Jeremy, "Septuagintalisms, Semitic Interference, and the Original Language of the Book of Judith," in *Studies in the Greek Bible: essays in honor of Francis T. Gignac, S.J*, ed. Jeremy Corley, Vincent Skemp (Washington DC: Catholic Biblical Association, 2008), 65–96.

Dorival, Gilles, "Autour des Titres des Psaumes," *RevSR* 73 (1999), 165–176.

Dorival, Gilles, "L'appartenance des Psaumes de Salomon au canon biblique," in *The Psalms of Solomon: Collected Essays*, ed. Felix Albrecht, Kenneth Atkinson, Patrick Pouchelle, Parabiblica 1 (Tübingen: Mohr Siebeck, 2023), 147–158.

Embry, Brad, "The Psalms of Solomon and the New Testament: Intertextuality and the Need for a Re-Evaluation," *JSP* 13 (2002), 99–136.

Erzberger, Johanna, "Changing Contexts: Psalms of Solomon 11 and Its Parallel in Baruch 4:5–5:9," *The Psalms of Solomon: Texts, Contexts, and Intertexts*, ed. G. Antony Keddie, Patrick Pouchelle, Kenneth Atkinson, Early Judaism and Its Literature 54 (Atlanta: SBL, 2021), 35–56.

Frankenberg, Wilhelm, *Die Datierung der Psalmen Salomo's. Ein Beitrag zur jüdischen Geschichte*, BZAW 1 (Giessen: J. Ricker, 1896).

Gebhardt, Oscar von, *ΨΑΛΜΟΙ ΣΟΛΟΜΩΝΤΟΣ: Die Psalmen Salomo's zum ersten Male mit Benutzung der Athoshandschriften und des Codex Casanatensis herausgegeben* (Leipzig: Hinrichs, 1895).

Geiger, Eduard Ephraem, *Der Psalter Salomo's erklärt und herausgegeben* (Augsburg: Wolffisch, 1871).

Gentry, Peter J. "The Greek Psalter and the καίγε Tradition," in *The Old Greek Psalter*, ed. R. J. V. Hiebert, C. E. Cox, and P. J. Gentry (Sheffield: Academic Press, 2001), 74–97.

Goldingay, John and David Payne, *Isaiah 40-55*, Volume II, ICC (London & New York: T&T Clark, 2006).

Gordley, Matthew E., "Psalms of Solomon as Solomonic Discourse: The Nature and Function of Attribution to Solomon in a Pseudonymous Psalm Collection," *JSP* 25 (2015), 52–88.

Greenspoon, Leonard J., "Recensions, Revision, Rabbinics: Dominique Barthélemy and Early Developments in the Greek Traditions," *Textus* 15 (1990), 153–167.

Hacham, Noah, "Where Does the Shekhinah Dwell? Between Dead Sea Sect, Diaspora Judaism and Rabbinic Literature," in *The Dead Sea Scrolls in Context: Integrating the Dead Sea Scrolls in the Study of Ancient Texts, Languages, and Cultures*, vol. 1, ed. A. Lange, E. Tov, M. Weigold, (Brill: Leiden, 2011), 399–412.

Haelewyck, Jean-Claude, "Le canon de l'Ancien Testament dans la tradition syriaque," in *L'Ancien Testament en syriaque*, ed. Françoise Briquel Chatonnet, Philippe Le Moigne, Études syriaques 5 (Paris: Geuthner, 2008), 141–171.

Hengel, Martin, *Judentum und Hellenismus: Studien zu ihrer Begegnung unter besonderer Berücksichtigung Palästinas bis zur Mitte des 2 Jh.s v. Chr.* (Tübingen: Mohr Siebeck, 1969); ET by John Bowden: *Judaism and Hellenism: Studies in Their Encounter in Palestine during the Early Hellenistic Period* (London: SCM Press; Philadelphia: Fortress, 1974).

Hilgenfeld, Adolf, *Messias Iudaeorum: libris eorum paulo ante et paulo post Christum natum conscriptis illustratus* (Leipzig: Sumptu Fuesiano, 1869).

Himmelfarb, Martha, "The Pseudepigrapha in Greek: Translation, Composition, and the Diaspora," in *The Old Testament Pseudepigrapha: Fifty Years of the Pseudepigrapha Section of the SBL*, ed. Matthias Henze, Liv Ingeborg Lied, Early Judaism and Its Literature 50 (SBL 2019), 263–286.

Hughes, Julie, *Scriptural Allusions and Exegesis in the Hodayot*, STDJ 59 (Leiden: Brill, 2006).

Janz, Timothy, *Deuxième livre d'Esdras*, La Bible d'Alexandrie XI 2 (Paris: Cerf, 2010).

Jonge, Marinus de, *Outside the Old Testament* (Cambridge: CUP, 1985).

Joosten, Jan, "The Prayer of Azariah (DanLXX 3): Sources and Origin," in *Septuagint and Reception*, ed. Johann Cook, VTS 127 (Leiden: Brill, 2009), 5–16.

Joosten, Jan, "The Interpretation of Deuteronomy 29:17–18 in the Hellenistic Period. Septuagint, Qumran and Parabiblical Literature," in *The Dynamics of Language and Exegesis at Qumran*, ed. D. Dimant, R. G. Kratz, FAT 35 (Tübingen: Mohr Siebeck, 2009), 107–120.

Joosten, Jan, "Reflections on the Original Language of the Psalms of Solomon," in *The Psalms of Solomon: Language, History, Theology*, ed. E. Bons, P. Pouchelle, Early Judaism and Its Literature 40 (Atlanta: SBL, 2015), 31-47.

Joosten, Jan, "The Origin of the Septuagint Canon," in *Die Septuaginta – Orte und Intentionen*, ed. Siegfried Kreuzer, Martin Meiser, Marcus Sigismund, WUNT 361 (Tübingen: Mohr Siebeck, 2016), 688-699.

Joosten, Jan, "New light on Proto-Theodotion. The Psalms of Solomon and the Milieu of the *Kaige* Recension," in *Die Septuaginta – Geschichte, Wirkung, Relevanz*, ed. Martin Meiser et al., WUNT 405 (Tübingen: Mohr Siebeck, 2018), 304–315.

Joosten, Jan, "The verb συνετίζω 'to instruct' in the Septuagint Psalms and beyond" in *"Må de nu förklara..." Om bibeltexter, religion, litteratur. Festskrift för Staffan Olofsson*, ed. Rosmari Lillas-Schuil et al. (Göteborg: LIR, 2018), 105–113.

Joosten, Jan, "The Accusation of Incest in Psalms of Solomon 8:9. Apologetics, Halakha, and Exegesis," in *Tempel, Lehrhaus, Synagoge. Orte jüdischen Lernens und Lebens. Festschrift für Wolfgang Kraus*, ed. Christian Eberhart et al. (Paderborn: Ferdinand Schöningh, 2020), 205–215.

Kamenetzky, Abraham S. "*Tehillot Shelomoh*," *Hashiloah* 13 (1904), 43–55, 149–159.

Keddie, G. Anthony, "Poverty and Exploitation in the Psalms of Solomon: At the Intersection of Sapiential and Apocalyptic Discourses," in *The Psalms of Solomon: Texts, Contexts, and Intertexts*, ed. G. Antony Keddie, Patrick Pouchelle, Kenneth Atkinson, Early Judaism and Its Literature 54 (Atlanta: SBL, 2021), 81–110.

Kim, Kyoung-Shik, *God Will Judge Each One According to Works (Judgment According to Works and Psalm 62 in Early Judaism and the New Testament* (Berlin: De Gruyter, 2010).

Kloppenborg, John S., "Dating Theodotos (CIJ II 1404)," *JJS* 51 (2000), 243–280.

Kraft, Robert "Reassessing the Impact of Barthélemy's *Devanciers* Forty Years Later," *BIOSCS* 37 (2004), 1-28.

Kugelmeier, Christoph, "Bibel, Papyri und Philosophen: Beobachtungen zur Geschichte hellenistischer Abstraktbegriffe," in *Septuagint*

*Vocabulary. Pre-History, Usage, Reception*, ed. Eberhard Bons, Jan Joosten (Atlanta: SBL, 2011), 25–44.

Lange, Armin and Matthias Weigold, *Biblical Quotations and Allusions in Second Temple Jewish Literature* (Göttingen: Vandenhoeck & Ruprecht, 2011), 23–34.

Lattke, Michaël, "Die Psalmen Salomos: Orte und Intentionen," in *Die Septuaginta - Orte und Intentionen*, ed. Siegfried Kreuzer, Martin Meiser, Marcus Sigismund, WUNT 361 (Tübingen: Mohr Siebeck, 2016), 78–95.

Marcovich, Miroslav, *Iustini Martyris Dialogus cum Tryphone* (Berlin & New York NY: De Gruyter, 1997).

Momigliano, Arnaldo, *On Pagans, Jews, and Christians* (Middletown CT: Wesleyan University Press, 1987).

Kabasele Mukenge, André, *L'unité du livre de Baruch* (Paris : Gabalda, 1998).

Munnich, Olivier, "La Septante des Psaumes et le groupe *kaige*," *VT* 33 (1983), 75–89.

Muraoka, Takamitsu, *A Greek-English Lexicon of the Septuagint* (Leuven: Peeters, 2009).

Najman, Hindy, *Seconding Sinai: The Development of Mosaic Discourse in Second Temple Judaism*, JSJS 77 (Leiden: Brill, 2003).

Newman, Judith, "The Democratization of Kingship in Wisdom of Solomon," in *The Idea of Biblical Interpretation: Essays in Honor of James L. Kugel*, ed. Hindy Najman and Judith Newman, SJSJ 83 (Leiden: Brill, 2003), 309–328.

Olofsson, Staffan, "The Kaige Group and the Septuagint Book of Psalms," in *IX Congress of the International Organization for Septuagint and Cognate Studies: Cambridge 1995*, ed. Bernard A. Taylor (Atlanta: Scholars, 1997), 189–230.

Parsons, Peter J., "The Scripts and their Date" in, *The Greek Minor Prophets Scroll from Nahal Hever (8HevXIIgr)*, ed. Emanuel Tov, The Seiyal Collection 1, DJD 8 (Oxford: Clarendon Press, 1990), 19–38.

Pearce, Sarah, "Jerusalem as 'Mother-City' in the Writings of Philo of Alexandria," in *Negotiating Diaspora: Jewish Strategies in the Roman Empire*, ed. John M. G. Barclay (T&T Clark, 2004), 19–37.

Peintner (Plangger), Stefanie and Georg Fischer, "ἀποικία κτλ," in *Historical and Theological Lexicon of the Septuagint*, ed. Eberhard Bons (Tübingen: Mohr Siebeck, 2020), 937-954.

Perles, Felix, "Zur Erklärung der Psalmen Salomos," *OLZ* 5 (1902), 269–282, 335–342, 365–372.

Pesch, W., "Die Abhängigkeit des 11. Salomonischen Psalms vom letzten Kapitel des Buches Baruch," *ZAW* 67 (1955), 251–263.

Pietersma, Albert "David in the Greek Psalms," *VT* 30 (1980), 213–226.

Pouchelle, Patrick, "Critique textuelle et traduction du treizième Psaume de Salomon," *JSJ* 42 (2011), 508–530

Pouchelle, Patrick, *Dieu éducateur: Une nouvelle approche d'un concept de la théologie biblique entre Bible Hébraïque, Septante et littérature grecque classique*, FAT II 77 (Tübingen: Mohr Siebeck, 2015).

Pouchelle, Patrick, "Prayers for being disciplined: Notes on παιδεύω and παιδεία in the Psalms of Solomon," in *The Psalms of Solomon: Language, History, Theology*, ed. Eberhard Bons, Patrick Pouchelle, Early Judaism and Its Literature 40 (Atlanta: SBL, 2015), 115–132.

Pouchelle, Patrick, "The Simple Bare Necessities: Is *Pss. Sol.* 5 a Wisdom Prayer ?" in *Tracing Sapiential Traditions in Ancient Judaism*, ed. Hindy Najman, J.-S. Rey, E. J. C. Tigchelaar, JSJS 174 (Leiden: Brill, 2016), 138–154.

Pouchelle, Patrick, "Flatterers, Whisperers, and Other Hypocrites: New Denominations for Sinners in the Writings of the Second Temple Period," in *New Vistas on Early Judaism and Christianity: From Enoch to Montréal and Back*, ed. L. DiTommaso, G. Oegema (London: Bloomsbury, 2016), 234–250.

Pouchelle, Patrick, "ἀνθρωπάρεσκος," in *Historical and Theological Lexicon of the Septuagint*, ed. Eberhard Bons (Tübingen: Mohr Siebeck, 2020), 737–744.

Pouchelle, Patrick, "Les scribes à l'œuvre dans les Psaumes de Salomon," *Henoch* 42 (2020), 344–359.

Pouchelle, Patrick, "The First Greek Quotation of the Psalms of Solomon Ever Found and its Importance For the History of the Reception of this Text," *The Psalms of Solomon: Collected Essays*, ed. Felix Albrecht, Kenneth Atkinson, Patrick Pouchelle, Parabiblica 1 (Tübingen: Mohr Siebeck, 2023), 131–146.

Reeser, Chad, "The Use of Isaiah in Psalm of Solomon 11 and Mark 1:1-15," draft paper published on academia.edu.

Remaud, Michel, *Évangile et tradition rabbinique* (Bruxelles: Lessius, 2003).

Ryle, Herbert and Montague James, *Ψαλμοὶ Σολομῶντος. Psalms of the Pharisees, Commonly Called the Psalms of Solomon* (Cambridge: CUP, 1891).

Samuel, Harald, "Albert Renovanz: „*Tehillim shelli-Shelomo* - Die Psalmen Salomo's ins Hebräische übersetzt"," *leqach* 9 (2009), 79–117.

Schürer, Emil, *The History of the Jewish People in the Age of Jesus Christ (175 B. C. - A. D. 135)*, English Version Revised and Edited by Geza Vermes, Fergus Millar, Martin Goodman (Edinburgh: T&T Clark, 1986).

Seeligmann, Isaac L., "Yerushalaim be-Mahshevet ha-Yehadut ha-Hellenistit," in idem, *Studies in Biblical Literature*, ed. Avi Hurvitz, Sara Japhet, Emanuel Tov (Jerusalem: Magnes, 1996), 396–410.

*Septuaginta Deutsch. Erläuterungen und Kommentare zum griechischen Alten Testament*, ed. Wolfgang Kraus, Martin Karrer (Stuttgart: Deutsche Bibelgesellschaft, 2011).

Sharon, Nadav, *Judea under Roman Domination. The First Generation of Statelessness and Its Legacy*, Early Judaism and Its Literature 46 (Atlanta: SBL, 2017).

Spicq, Ceslas, *Theological Lexicon of the New Testament* (Peabody MA: Hendrickson, 1994).

Stein, Menahem, "*Mizmorey Shelomoh*," in *Hasepharim Hahitsonim*, Vol. I, 2, ed. A. Kahana (Tel Aviv: Meqorot, 1936/37), 431–462.

Strack, Hermann L. and Paul Billerbeck, *Kommentar zum Neuen testament aus Talmud und Midrasch*, I–IV (München: Beck, 1926–28).

Swete, Henry B., *An Introduction to the Old Testament in Greek*, revised by Richard R. Ottley (Cambridge: CUP, 1914).

Tomson, Peter, *'Voor één dag genoeg': het brood, het Woord en de wetenschap* (Brussels: Universitaire Faculteit voor Protestantse Godgeleerdheid, 1993).

Tov, Emanuel, *The Greek Minor Prophets Scroll from Nahal Hever (8HevXIIgr)*, The Seiyal Collection 1, DJD 8 (Oxford: Clarendon Press, 1990).

Trafton, Joseph, *The Syriac Version of the Psalms of Solomon: A Critical Evaluation*, SCS 11 (Atlanta: Scholars Press, 1985).

Trafton, Joseph, "What Would David Do? Messianic Expectation and Surprise in Ps. Sol. 17," in *The Psalms of Solomon: Language, History, Theology*, ed. Eberhard Bons, Patrick Pouchelle, Early Judaism and Its Literature 40 (Atlanta: SBL, 2015), 155–174.

Ulrich, Eugene, *The Biblical Qumran Scrolls*, VTS 134 (Leiden: Brill, 2010).

Unnik, Willem C. van *Das Selbstverständnis der jüdischen Diaspora in der hellenistisch-römischen Zeit,* aus dem Nachlaß herausgegeben und bearbeitet von Pieter Willem van der Horst (Leiden: Brill, 1993).

Viteau, Joseph, *Les Psaumes de Salomon* (Paris: Letouzey & Ané, 1911).

Wellhausen, Julius, *Die Pharisäer und die Sadducäer. Eine Untersuchung zur inneren jüdischen Geschichte* (Greifswald: Bamberg, 1874)

Werline, Rodney A., "The Psalms of Solomon and the Ideology of Rule," in *Conflicted Boundaries in Wisdom and Apocalypticism*, ed. Benjamin G. Wright III, Lawrence M. Wills; SBLSymS 35 (Atlanta: SBL, 2005), 69–87.

Werline, Rodney A., "The Formation of the Pious Person in the Psalms of Solomon," in *The Psalms of Solomon: Language, History, Theology*, ed. Eberhard Bons, Patrick Pouchelle, Early Judaism and Its Literature 40 (Atlanta: SBL, 2015), 133–154.

Xeravits, Geza, *"Take Courage, O Jerusalem…" Studies in the Psalms of Baruch 4–5,* Deuterocanonical and Cognate Literature Studies, 25 (Berlin: De Gruyter 2015).

Youngblood, Kevin, J. "Lamentations," in *The T&T Clark Companion to the Septuagint,* ed. James K. Aitken (London/New York: Bloomsbury T&T Clark, 2015), 500–519.

Zurawski, Jason, "Solomonic Paideia: Divine Pedagogy in the Psalms of Solomon and the Book of Wisdom," in *The Psalms of Solomon: Collected Essays*, ed. Felix Albrecht, Kenneth Atkinson, Patrick Pouchelle, Parabiblica 1 (Tübingen: Mohr Siebeck, 2023), 85–100.

# Index of scriptural passages (including Psalms of Solomon)

# Index of Greek words

# Table of Contents